The Swing Set

the best days are yet to come

Mary Ellen Dirksen

Editorial input by
Tracy Kirby, Dori Quam and Jon Walker

To Darlene
you are the joy
of the Lord!
♥ M.E.

ME & FRIENDS PUBLISHING CO., LLC | SIOUX FALLS, SD

ME & Friends Publishing Co., LLC
Sioux Falls, South Dakota

strongrightarm.com

Scriptures taken from the Holy Bible, New International Version®, NIV®. Copyright © 1973, 1978, 1984, 2011 by Biblica, Inc.™ Used by permission of Zondervan. All rights reserved worldwide. www.zondervan.com The "NIV" and "New International Version" are trademarks registered in the United States Patent and Trademark Office by Biblica, Inc.™

ISBN 978-0-9970076-0-2 (Print)
ISBN 978-0-9970076-1-9 (Digital)

Printed in the United States of America

This book is dedicated to…
my Lord and Savior Jesus Christ;
my family;
and the millions of people bound by chains of anxiety, depression, addiction and fear.

Come to me, all you who are weary and burdened, and I will give you rest. Take my yoke upon you and learn from me, for I am gentle and humble at heart, and you will find rest for your souls. For my yoke is easy and my burden is light.

~ Says Jesus to us, as told in Matthew 11:28-29.

Prologue

In the parable of the five loaves and two fish, a little boy gives to Jesus the little he has and watches as the Lord multiplies it into a feast fit for thousands.

So often I've felt overwhelmed by a longing to offer, and disappointment in lacking, anything substantial for God to use. Then I remember the story of the little boy who with only his loaves and his fish helps to feed a multitude.

Reflecting on the years of my life and reading the words of Jesus, who spoke in simple stories, it occurred to me that perhaps I do have something to offer. This, my story.

My story isn't at all about what I did or did not do, but rather, it is about Jesus, and what He can and will do with the little we have to offer if only we are willing.

It is my greatest hope that in reading this book, you too will see Him at work in your own story. That you will see the evidence of the divine in those ordinary and extraordinary moments collectively called "life," and that you will share with others the gifts of joy, hope and wisdom you acquired in those moments in the way that only you can do. Blessings on your journey, dear friend.

~~~

The Catalyst

Something brewed in the air as my then-fiancé and I talked one sunny afternoon in my apartment. Up to that point, we had talked only about the mundanities of daily life, like where to eat dinner that evening, until out of nowhere I blurted, "What is your passion in life?"

He looked at me quizzically for a moment, answered and then asked the same question of me. I paused for a bit. I had never considered the question. The question had simply burst out of me.

Finally, a singular thought crystallized.

"I want to know how God is involved in our everyday lives *today*. I know what He did thousands of years ago in the stories in the Bible, but what is He doing in our lives right now? I want to see it."

I recall those words in that moment clear as a bell, and I believe God heard me speak those words and that they meant something to Him. It was as if those words shot through the heavens like lightning and struck deep into the heart of God as He sat on His throne.

The Bible tells us that we can be blinded to the truths of God and the blindness will afflict us until God in His mercy opens our eyes and gives us greater awareness of Him. I had never read about this in the Bible. I only knew there was something more going on out there and I wanted to witness it.

I see now that, yes, I was blind to the greater truths of God. And I see now that if God had not opened my eyes, I might not have survived what was to follow.

Rob and Me

My nine-year-old daughter, Kate, dreamed about my brother Rob the night before I started writing this story. In her dream, my husband, our three daughters and I sat together around the dinner table. My cell phone rang. It was Rob calling to say he was coming back. She said I was so excited. She couldn't quite describe how excited I was to receive that phone call.

If only he were to come back.

~ ~ ~

The day Rob died, the trees lining the street near his home seemed so tall. It was as if I was suddenly smaller and the world around me was warped to an oversized dimension. It was scarier and darker than I'd ever seen it. Those towering trees formed a sinister canopy high above the fire trucks and police cars in the street below. Why were those trees so tall?

We stepped out of the car. I stood there, twenty-five years old, feeling like a little girl lost and alone.

~ ~ ~

Rob had called me, eight years before he died, breathless. I held the phone, twisting the cord around my finger, lying on my parents' bed as I listened to the words spilling out of Rob. "Mary, big news. Dirksen is single. I think you two are going to get married."

Never mind I'd never met Dirksen, and that Dirksen was a sophomore in college while I was a few days away from my high school senior prom. Rob just knew.

~ ~ ~

The first time I saw Dirksen, I thought three things: (1) He seems kind. (2) He seems to be going somewhere exciting. (3) I want to go, too.

We started dating my freshman year of college. We were engaged five months and two days after our first date. And we were married a year later, a short two years and two months after Rob's phone call. Rob really did know.

On that sticky, hot morning in the summer of 2005, Dirksen and I stood together under those towering trees outside the home where we learned Rob had taken his life. I was so confused. The person who died that day, they said his name was Rob and that he was my brother, but my mind resisted this. It couldn't be Rob dead in that house. The brother I knew had hope. The brother I knew believed anything was possible. Who was this Rob who died? I didn't understand. I didn't understand.

~ ~ ~

It was a Sunday morning, July 17, 2005. My husband, our four-year-old daughter, Rachel, and I planned to attend my in-laws' church, where his grandfather was to preach.

I awoke to pounding on the back door below the bedroom. My eyes opened to intense sunlight filtering through the sheer white canopy overhead. The sunlight was unusually beautiful, as if its rays were dancing into the room.

But louder pounding on the door jolted my thoughts away from the sunlight and a chilly nervousness washed over me. I ran down the stairs. Maybe it was my dad coming to talk to me about last night. This gets confusing. Bear with me.

We dined at my parents' the night before; my parents, Rob and me and our families. After dinner, Rob and I fought. Something near Rob was about to fall and break. I called out to warn him, yet he did nothing. He only stared at me blankly. Frustrated, I screamed at him, "What is wrong with you?" And not in a way that invited an answer.

He stormed off. He was going to leave without even saying goodbye. Rachel, my little girl, ran after him, yelling, "Uncle Rob, play ball with me! You promised me you would!" She chased after him down the steps, carrying an oversized, red playground ball almost as big as she was. Rob was so moved by her plea that he stayed. They played catch one last time.

As we prepared to leave later that evening, Rob walked over to me. As we stood together in the kitchen, he took his huge hand—big enough to palm a basketball with ease—and he palmed my pregnant belly. "Your belly's as big as a basketball, Mary." We all laughed. This is the last thing Rob ever said to me.

We parted that evening as friends, our explosive disagreement defused by a tender-hearted little girl.

I shouldn't have lashed out at Rob that night, and I knew it as soon as I awoke to the pounding on the door. I stumbled down the stairs half-awake and saw my mom waiting outside the back door for me to let her inside. She burst in, rushed to the living room and sat on the arm of the couch. I sat down, too, and waited for her to speak.

The words tumbled out. "Rob hurt himself," she said. My mom was heading over to his house. Rob's wife had called her in a state of panic. My mom thought his wife said Rob had an accident with a saw, which we would soon discover was nowhere near the truth. I still wonder why we sat down on the couch for that brief interchange.

It was going to be okay. I knew it. Everything can be fixed, I thought. For some reason, my mind went back to all the parking tickets I had talked my way out of in college. In my mind, in my world, up to that point everything was negotiable.

I ran upstairs to tell my husband that Rob was injured. My husband and I whisked our little girl out of bed in her pajamas, piled into the car and drove off toward Rob's house.

It all seemed better for a moment. I was relieved it wasn't my dad at the door. I was sure he had come to rail on me about my argument with Rob the night before.

It sounds strange, now, when I reflect on how entangled our family dynamics were at the time. Rob and I were adults, after all, and siblings do have arguments. But around that time, our family was in turmoil, and anything was possible. It was a strange time. From talking to others who have a loved one suffering from a mental illness, I've learned that strained family dynamics are commonplace. Our very normal family had become very abnormal.

When we arrived at Rob's house, police cars and fire trucks already lined the streets. My father-in-law, a fireman, was there, too. He heard the call come across the radio on his way home from work that morning and recognized the address. The situation was not good. Rob had taken his life that morning and was dead by the time the ambulance arrived.

~ ~ ~

Rob left a note, and in many ways questions remain about even the simplest elements of the note. The note was started in pen, written in Rob's tight, angled handwriting. About halfway through the note you could see the pen was running out of ink. The words started to fade. Rob found a pencil and used it to finish the note. The note was written half in ink, half in pencil.

I still find it so strange that a man who could no longer bear the weight of this world still had enough fight to finish writing that note.

I imagine that if I were writing a note and the pen ran out of ink, it might have given me pause, forcing me to reflect on what I was doing.

I wonder what was going through Rob's mind that morning as he wrote that note and then was looking for a pencil when the pen ran out of ink. That was a moment of decision, and in that moment he was choosing between life and death.

After all these years, the whole thing doesn't make sense. I've experienced enough of my own inner angst and seen it in others that I have a measure of understanding of what Rob experienced, but I don't understand in full what was going on inside Rob's mind that morning. He wasn't thinking rationally. But I still feel compelled to ask: Why didn't he stop when that pen ran out of ink?

~ ~ ~

We waited in a neighbor's living room while the first responders did what they needed to do over at Rob's house. As we stood together in silence I couldn't get it out of my mind that I had to go see Rob's body. I turned toward the neighbor's back door time and time again, wanting to walk the few steps over to Rob's house. It seems morbid now, but I yearned to lay down beside him just like I used to when we slept on the outside under the stars as little kids and I grew afraid and clung to him.

I wanted to see the house exactly as Rob saw it in the minutes before he died. Maybe there was a clue of some sort, a tidbit or a memento that might help me understand. I couldn't figure out what was happening. Maybe something at the scene would help me understand.

My husband talked to the first responders. The scene was not good. He persuaded me not to go over to Rob's house, so I did not. I am thankful now that I did not.

~ ~ ~

The ambulance removed Rob's body to deliver it to the coroner. He was gone. The confusion remained as my family stood on the driveway outside Rob's house. We needed a different base camp. We planned to meet at my parents' house a few miles out of town. Just like last night, only this time Rob wouldn't be there.

But first, Rob's cat Jingles needed food. I would go get the cat food. It was important to have something to do.

The grocery store was frigid on that hot summer day. I wasn't dressed for it. I must have had on a tank top. My shoulders felt cold.

Jingles' cat food dropped like a bag of rocks onto the floor as I pulled it off the shelf. Bending my knees, I tried using my legs to lift the bag, but my pregnant belly pressed uncomfortably against my knees. Awkwardly, I dragged the bag of cat food, twisting and turning the bag until it rested on the rack underneath the grocery cart.

The cat pictured on the bag was adorable, really, with its paw playfully sneaking forward as if ready to pounce. It lay there on the rack on the bottom of the grocery cart, the picture of that playful cat staring up at me.

I waited at the checkout, leaning against the cart. Glancing to my left, I noticed a mother and daughter one checkout lane over. "Did her brother die by suicide today?" I wondered. Probably not. I looked to my right to see a gray-haired man with a mustache. I doubted whether he had lost someone that day, but then again I probably didn't look that way either. I was just a pregnant woman buying cat food, and the cat on that bag looked so darn playful there was no way someone had just died. It made no sense.

~ ~ ~

We were cat lovers from as far back as I can remember. Our farm cats fended for themselves for the most part, save for table scraps every now and then.

Kittens were a big deal. They marked the arrival of spring. We stalked the mama kitty as her belly grew larger and her teats formed moist droplets, knowing she would deliver soon. Mama kitty was a creature of habit. She usually settled on a spot in the hay mow in the white barn on our farmyard, except for the one year she nestled her newborn kittens in a hole in one of the box elder trees lining the gravel driveway. Not a good choice if I recall correctly. I think the coons got that litter.

Every spring at least four kittens arrived, and most of them survived, for awhile at least. Rob and I were opinionated and passionate about kittens. Finally, in an effort to maintain sibling relations, we instituted a Kitten Draft.

The Kitten Draft was a serious affair, conducted with small scraps of paper on which Rob wrote numbers representing draft picks. One of us drew a piece of paper from a baseball cap. A "1" signified the first and fourth round draft pick, while a "2" signified a second and third round draft pick. Rob imposed a designated waiting period between each draft pick for maximum drama, along with other rules I can't seem to recall except that they made the experience even more amazing.

Oh, how we loved our kitties. We were not allowed to bring cats inside the house, but that seemed more a suggestion than a bright-line rule. On summer days, Rob and I sneaked the kittens into the air-conditioned living room, where we would watch television under a mound of blankets.

Nothing was cuter than little kitten faces peeking out from under blankets during Saturday morning cartoons. It didn't last long. Mom wised up when she saw us lying under mounds of blankets in the middle of summer.

Rob had a way of softening the hardest hearts, and by my eleventh birthday, he somehow convinced our mother to let us have a kitten in the house. Our first and only house cat was formally named Skumpky Wumpky, with a nickname Wumpsker.

Wumpsker was medium-orange with cream accents, and looked strikingly like Jingles, Rob's house cat who my little girl Rachel liked carrying around by the tail because to a three-year-old a tail appears to be made for that purpose. Jingles ran and hid behind the entertainment center whenever Rachel showed up at Rob's house.

~ ~ ~

I met the others at my parents' house after the run to the grocery store for Jingles' cat food. The ceiling fan on my parents' patio twirled, but it seemed slower than usual, as if suspended in time.

My parents and our pastor joined me on the patio, where we sat together on wicker chairs around a large, round, glass-topped table. It must have been late afternoon by then, otherwise pastor would have been at church.

My mind jumped into overdrive as I traced the pattern of wicker underneath the glass table top, and I knew then what I hadn't known before: Rob was depressed and suffering from an anxiety disorder. Mental illness.

I had known he wasn't dressing well, that he looked unshaven, that he was irritable and that this was causing turmoil in our family. I had known he wasn't leaving the house, that he didn't take interest in life like he used to, and that his worldview had become pessimistic.

But I had never really known anyone who suffered from depression, actual depression, especially not someone handsome and capable like my brother.

He was Rob, after all. The older brother who read the encyclopedia in the summertime to increase his intellect, who ran up and down the highway alongside our house wearing shoes designed to increase his vertical jump. If he could give up on life, where was the hope for the rest of us?

Sitting on the patio with our pastor, I apologized to my parents. I reflected on so many phone calls...so many phone calls...leading up to that day. On those phone calls I had yelled at them, expressing disgust with how they were handling my brother. I told them they were babying Rob. That they needed to give him a swift kick in the butt. That they needed to... I can't remember all the ways we had disagreed. In that instant I realized in the days leading up to Rob's death my family had needed much grace, and that I had not extended it, especially to Rob.

If I had known he was depressed, how much differently would I have treated him?

My mind was busy at work on this. If only he hadn't yelled at me when I yelled at him. If only he had told me he was sad. I suppose he was trying all that time, but I couldn't hear beyond his words. My heart had been hardened toward him. I was disappointed with him. How could someone with that much potential not pull it together? Rob's struggles, which to me seemed a simple matter of Rob growing up and assuming responsibility, instead were crystallized into a struggle for his very life.

~ ~ ~

When I was a junior in high school, I bought a gleaming, marshmallow-white puffer jacket with a hood. The Eddie Bauer tag vowed it would keep me warm in temperatures as low as eighty degrees below zero. It was an extra-large, far too big for me, but it was the only one left and I knew it was destined to be mine.

Rob called it "Marshmallow." The coat became like a pet in our family. Whenever I appeared wearing it, my family would remark, "Mary's wearing Marshmallow." Or, "Hey, there's Marshmallow."

At the age of twenty-seven, two years after Rob died, we moved across the country to Harrisburg, Pennsylvania. I knew one person in the area, but our paths didn't cross often. It seemed my only friends for a while were the gentleman and two women who worked at the Turkey Hill® gas station near our home. I visited them every morning, filling a 44-ounce plastic cup with ice cubes and diet soda, making small talk for a few minutes in a way that cheered me up.

That winter, I pulled Marshmallow out of storage to brace against the chill in the air. By that point, I was so tired and lonely I didn't care about much anymore. Rob's death and the questions surrounding it had taken its toll on me. The house was a mess, and I knew it, but I didn't have the energy to clean it up. I hadn't showered for several days, even those days when the kids had stomach flu and vomited in my hair at night, but still I just couldn't seem to care. It's painful to think back to that time.

The day I pulled out Marshmallow was the day I did not wear makeup in public. I had never, not even once, ventured out in public without makeup from age thirteen onward. Maybe it was a basic courtesy, a signal to the world I cared enough to try to look nice, or maybe it was a mask. Or perhaps a combination of the two.

For whatever reason, that chilly morning, in the cocoon of Marshmallow, I walked into the Turkey Hill gas station without makeup. Worse yet, I had been crying the night before and my eyes were swollen and red.

The kindly gentleman and the two women had become my friends. They looked at me in surprise. I remember seeing their faces and knowing I had crossed some sort of line, not for their sake but more so for mine. I didn't care anymore about how I looked. A little before Rob died, he stopped caring about his appearance. His dark brown hair was matted and mussed in odd patches, and not in a stylish way. He wasn't shaving. He wasn't sleeping well and so his eyes, too, were red. He wore dirty clothes.

I yelled at him for that.

The day of Rob's funeral, I sat at the vanity in my house applying makeup with a shaky hand. Extended family offered to help dress Rachel for the funeral. "What does Mary Ellen want her to wear?" they asked my husband, Jesse. I said the "F" word to Jesse when he asked. "Who cares what she wears?" I wanted to scream. My brother had just died, taken his life, and they wanted to know what she should wear to the funeral. They were trying to help, I know, and yet it burned me.

It burned me because in that moment, I realized Rob hadn't been careless about his appearance. He couldn't care because he was filled with other cares. He was so sad, so lost and confused by the expanse of darkness surrounding him that he couldn't bother himself with what he looked like. I understood in that split second while getting ready for his funeral.

And I understood, standing in that gas station so many months later, that in some shadowy sense, I had become my brother, not caring enough to wear makeup or to shower, so consumed by the black void inside me that I couldn't care about what I looked like.

The moment in the gas station jarred me back to some semblance of caring, of coping with reality, of pulling back from the brink and taking pains to shove down the cloud of darkness rising up inside me in order to function. I wish I could tell you I was driven by inner strength or courage or bravery, but that wasn't it. It was pride. I cared what others thought about me. I wanted people to admire my appearance. I wanted people to think I had inner strength. That day at the gas station, I realized maintaining the façade might require more work than it had in years past.

~ ~ ~

Premature. It all seemed premature. I was doing things I hadn't anticipated doing until at least in my late seventies. It was all happening way too soon.

We picked out music for his funeral. We chose a belt, khaki pants and shirt for the viewing. It was the brown leather belt we bought on a family trip to Thailand, a fake Polo Ralph Lauren belt that was starting to crack around the buckle.

It was the same pair of khakis and the same belt he wore to our college graduation a few years earlier. We graduated the same year, and celebrated at Valentino's Restaurant, which served the very best Sicilian cream spaghetti sauce in the world until it shuttered two weeks ago to make room for a corporate cell phone office.

I wonder now, in a very morbid thought, that perhaps it would be nice to see that belt and those khaki pants again. I suppose they are still intact after these ten years in a casket. It is funny what you wonder about when someone is gone.

It is sad to think back to his funeral. For all the years we loved Rob and cared for him, it all happened too fast and was too confusing to plan a parting that adequately expressed the impact he had on our lives. I mean, the funeral was nice and everything, but if we had known he would be leaving us we could have prepared something more representative of his life. His funeral should have been outspoken and energetic, yet private and deep, just like Rob. How could we have planned an ordinary funeral? I am so sorry Rob. I am so sorry. We just didn't have the time or the presence of mind to do it well enough to reflect the fullness of you.

At the viewing, my husband noticed Rob's fingernails. Rob must have started biting his nails again in the weeks before his death. He had stopped for awhile. I didn't notice his nails, because all I could see was Rob's outfit. Particularly that belt.

I felt little connection to Rob's body at the viewing. I touched his hand, but it was stiff and waxy, not the sweaty, warm hand I used to know so well. That wasn't really Rob anymore in the casket.

~ ~ ~

Rob and I often played in the dirt right where the lawn met the cornfield on our farmyard. We dug trenches in the dirt, piling the dirt into huge walls. When two of our childhood friends, Paul and Rachel, visited, we declared "dirt clod wars" between the girls and boys, hurling chunks of dirt at each other as we crouched in the trenches behind the walls of dirt.

A few years ago, my cousin Steven and I visited Gettysburg National Military Park. By happenstance, we visited on July 2, 2010, one hundred forty-seven years to the day since the start of the skirmish at Culp's Hill. It was fitting to visit Gettysburg with Steven, who reminds me of Rob in the very best ways.

National Park employees stood at the entrance to the visitor's center with all sorts of Civil War soldier regalia, including heavy woolen jackets and weapons. A cluster of kids stood in the middle of all that regalia, putting on uniforms oversized on their small frames while parents took pictures. Alongside them stood my cousin Steven, almost thirty years old and a towering 6 foot 5, putting on a uniform just the right size for his frame, belying that he was an oversized kid at heart. I couldn't help but think that a part of Rob was still with me that day.

Steven and I walked around the battlefields and stopped to hear a park ranger give a talk at Culp's Hill, a lesser known yet critical site in the Battle of Gettysburg.

The park ranger shared how the Union Army defended the Hill thanks to the foresight of an officer who directed his troops to build breastworks, temporary fortifications made of felled trees, rocks and earth.

This commanding officer was trained as a civil engineer and saw the value of creating a defensive position. He also knew how to build it. Historians credit the breastworks in large part for the victory on Culp's Hill with very few casualties on the Union side.

Steven and I walked our way down Culp's Hill through bramble and uneven terrain, envisioning the men building the breastworks. It reminded me of our days on the farm, when Rob and I constructed our own meager breastworks out of heavy black Iowa soil.

I wanted to call Rob, to share all I had learned from the park ranger that day at Gettysburg. I wanted to show him pictures of Steven in the soldier uniform alongside all those little kids, so we could laugh together and enjoy stories of Steven's awesomeness.

I wanted to tell him the fortifications we made to prepare for our dirt clod wars were called "breastworks," and that we actually kind of knew what we were doing.

I longed to share with him all my thoughts in those moments overlooking Culp's Hill, imagining soldiers who had fallen, thinking of all the sisters who had lost brothers in the Civil War and all the parents who lost sons. I wanted to tell him it got me thinking that I, too, lost a brother in battle, an internal conflict, except that the nation survived its battle on that steamy July day, while my brother did not.

We all know that chemical imbalance is one of the leading contributors to depression, anxiety and thoughts of suicide. Chemical imbalance is a widely accepted cause of depression. We are comfortable with chemical imbalance. We can measure it. We can see it. We can medicate it.

We know through research that oftentimes there is an increase in suicidal ideation from certain medications. Rob was taking anti-anxiety medication before he died but had stopped without consulting his physician. One of the risks of that medication was an increased risk of suicidal thoughts when going off the medication. Yes, with Rob, that seems to be more than a coincidence.

The next element to this whole equation is a bit trickier. Trickier in the sense it's definitely not commonly embraced, and further, because it doesn't seem to be as studied or researched as other aspects of the equation. It's the spiritual element, those forces of evil that cause or worsen depression, anxiety, fear and unhealthy thoughts about death or suicide.

The Bible tells us in Ephesians 6:12, "For our struggle is not against flesh and blood, but against the rulers, against the authorities, against the powers of this dark world and against the spiritual forces of evil in the heavenly realms."

Over the last few years, as I started to break free of my own struggles with depression and anxiety after Rob's death, the practical implications of this passage became eerily apparent through an undeniable and bizarre string of encounters.

The first occurred early in the summer a few years ago as I promoted a suicide prevention fundraiser in Sioux Falls. I arrived at Falls Park along the Big Sioux River for an early-morning news interview. The reporter informed me that, sadly, just a few hours earlier a young medical student had taken his life in the parking lot just across the water.

A few weeks later, while on vacation in Yankton, South Dakota, I saw a man at the corner of a busy intersection, sitting on a retaining wall, hunched over casually, but with his arms held up and blood running from his wrists down his arms. I called 911 to report the incident. It was terribly unsettling. My lungs panicked and my breathing rippled in uncomfortably short spurts. My stomach churned and cramped in anxiety. I couldn't fall asleep that night. I was terrorized.

A few weeks later in Spokane, Washington, my mom and I pulled up to our hotel to find a cadre of cop cars just outside the lobby. After settling into our room, I walked back to the lobby and pulled aside an officer. I just knew someone in the hotel was attempting suicide. I could feel it in my bones. Sure enough, the officer confirmed a man was locked in his room and threatening to take his life. He had told his mom over the phone, and she called the police. They arrived in time to prevent his act.

A short while later, at a fundraising event, a woman made a beeline for me from across a crowded room to introduce herself. She was strange. Her eyes darted back and forth. She told me both of her parents had died by suicide. I tried politely to disengage from the conversation, but she seemed intent on attaching herself to me. The encounter made me feel very afraid.

It was everywhere, so strange, as if it was following me around. I felt the evil, the strange way that it had attached to me. It paralyzed me with fear. Over the years, I've shared these incidents with a few people. Quite honestly, I think they think I'm weird. In fact, a few of them have avoided me since.

By sharing this, I may alienate some of you or may be castigated as strange. But I know what I saw and I know what happened to Rob, and I know there is more to all of this than simply levels of a chemical in the blood or simple thought patterns. Yes, it is all those things. Of course it's our physical bodies, of course it's our thought patterns, and of course we need to talk through it with professionals.

But there is more to it than that. There is, as the Bible warns, an evil that prowls around as a devouring lion, ready to steal, kill and destroy. It is not coincidence that after Satan entered Judas and incited him to betray Jesus, Judas then hung himself. He hung himself for shame and hopelessness. Luke 22, Matthew 27. It is not coincidence that when Jesus cast demons out of a man and into a herd of pigs, the pigs immediately ran into a lake and drowned. Luke 8.

Rob was not possessed, because Rob believed in Jesus as his savior, and, as believers, we are filled with the Holy Spirit and sealed off. But believers can be afflicted by tormenting spirits that oppress our spirits and incite fear, depression, and a host of other negative thoughts and emotions. We battle not against flesh and blood, but against powers and principalities of darkness, and I believe that is exactly what Rob battled in those days leading up to that July morning.

~ ~ ~

I barely slept the night he died. I was terrified, lying awake in bed. When I finally drifted off I suffered from dreams so awful I was afraid even to sleep. I was in terror both awake and asleep.

The terror persisted for weeks. I feared a burglar entering our bedroom and violently stabbing me and my family. I feared strange creatures lurking in our bedroom as I lay awake with both eyes scanning the darkness. I was five months pregnant and I feared the stress of grief was strangling the baby stirring in my belly. It did not. She was born healthy.

I would awaken in the dead of night, heart racing, tormented by graphic, violent dreams. The first dream, the night after he died, violent criminals knocked on our back door. When I opened the door, Rob's bloody, severed head lay at our back door. I'm sure there's all kinds of symbolism wrapped up in that one, but what prevails as important is the effect it had: How I struggled to breathe, pulling the blankets up high around me, making sure my back was to my husband.

"If my back is to my husband when I'm sleeping, no one can sneak up on me," I thought. This same thought impacted my sleep habits for years to follow. I slept much better—felt much safer—sleeping with my back to my husband. I was being prudent, you see. Keeping watch in order to warn my husband of the attacker whom I was convinced would someday assault us in the middle of the night.

The morning of the funeral, the family gathered in the basement of our church for a brief message by our pastor. He talked about Psalm 23, which tells us that even though we walk through the valley of the shadow of death, we should fear no evil, for goodness and mercy will follow us and we will dwell in the house of the Lord forever.

Up until that day I had never associated fear with death. But now I understood. I understood the significance of the statement that we should not fear even when walking in the shadow of death. And I understood the significance of being followed by goodness and mercy after lying awake at night fearing evil attacking me from behind. Yet I did not believe it, for I continued to sleep with my back to my husband.

~ ~ ~

It's strange because I thought I was fearless.

One day we heard sportscaster Bob Costas say that Jerry Rice's seasoned hands were forged in the brickyards alongside his dad, where Rice caught rough, heavy bricks all day long. Rice, the young blue-collar worker, would later become one of the greatest pass receivers in pro football history.

As soon as the sun rose the next morning, Rob and I gleefully ran out to the old pile of bricks next to the chicken coop, where we planned to forge our own small, stubby hands into those of a wide receiver.

Rob let me go first. I stood precariously atop a pile of old rubbish and lumber with exposed nails, catching bricks with my bare hands as Rob tossed them to me. There might have even been a mouse in that pile of rubbish. But none of it scared me at all that day.

~ ~ ~

Rob could get anyone to do anything. Even our ninety-year-old grandma.

Grandma Leta lived on the farm in a 1970s era ranch-style home, the kind with a brass chandelier and gold shag carpet, a few miles down the gravel road from our farmhouse. She cherished that chandelier, admiring it as she sat in the motorized recliner near her television set.

Grandma was a woman of faith who prayed for Rob and me. In high school Rob asked her to pray that he would grow taller. His goal was 6-foot-4. As Rob grew, his head rose ever closer that chandelier.

Eventually it occurred to Rob that he could rub his head on the bottom of the chandelier. Every time he visited grandma, he checked his progress by rubbing his head on that chandelier, marveling as more of his hair, and finally his scalp, rubbed against the cool brass. The prayers were working.

But then! But then grandma realized the oils from Rob's scalp were tarnishing the brass. She chastised Rob, but the more she chastised him, the more he rubbed his head on her light fixture. They reached détente when my grandma refused to pray for Rob's continued growth unless and until he stopped tarnishing her chandelier.

Rob indeed grew to 6-foot-4. At his peak he bench pressed 400 pounds. He could dunk a basketball by simply standing under the hoop and jumping up to stuff it through with both hands. Apparently this kind of dunk is difficult to achieve. He was proud of that dunk.

Rob was a gifted persuader who even managed to convince Grandma Leta to watch Michael Jordan play with the Chicago Bulls throughout the basketball season. He wouldn't take her word for it, though. Every morning after a televised Bulls game, Rob called and peppered her with questions about Jordan's statistics or a memorable play during the game to make sure she was watching. She took to the challenge and relished reporting in every morning after a game. They kept each other sharp.

~ ~ ~

If one word encapsulated an enduring passion of Rob's life it was this: Basketball. Anywhere, with anyone, he played basketball as much as he could.

We worked all summer on the farm, often at my Grandma Leta's acreage, where a basketball hoop was mounted over her garage door. In the summertime, after lunch we would shoot hoops, practicing our fade-away jumper before returning to the field. Iowa winters are harsh, so my dad installed a hoop inside the machine shed behind grandma's house so we could shoot hoops in the wintertime. When it was frigid cold, we burned corn cobs in a belching, black stove to heat the machine shed just enough so we could shoot hoops without having to wear gloves.

Through junior high and high school, Rob played basketball summer evenings in the park in Sibley, Iowa. The lights above the court let off a gentle buzz in the evenings, as moths and mosquitoes darted to and fro overhead. The evenings were beautiful. I would drink it all in, sitting on the grass by the court watching Rob play with his best friend, Jon, until our parents picked us up later that evening.

Something changed for Rob in the spring of 1998, the day our dear Grandma Helen died. She was sick with stomach cancer. We knew it at Christmas when Rob and I sat down for our last picture with her. Rob wrapped his  arms around both of us from behind, with our frail Grandma Helen grinning wide. Rob was a sophomore in college at the time, and I was a senior in high school.

Before she died, I drove the ten or so miles to the Sibley hospital every morning before school to visit and feed her the chocolate custard-filled long johns she could never otherwise have because of her diabetes. By early 1998, I had moved to Des Moines to work as a page in the Iowa House of Representatives. By the time she died in the middle of March, I had cried enough tears and relinquished enough of her that the actual death seemed a natural progression.

For Rob, it was different. He was in college, busy playing basketball and wrapped up in his own world as a student. Rob wasn't aware she was dying, or at least he hadn't absorbed the reality yet. My husband, then a friend of Rob's who lived with him in the dorms at the time, remembers the day Grandma Helen died. He saw Rob emerge from a stairwell with an ashen face and remembers him saying, "Dude, my grandma just died." It seemed from that moment, everything changed for Rob.

He wouldn't take his life for another seven years. But something was out of balance. Questions filled his mind: Why would God let someone we love die? Why did God have to take grandma to heaven? Why couldn't she stay with us here on Earth? Why? Why, why, why, why, why. On and on the questions replayed in Rob's mind.

Rob asked me these questions over and over and over again. My answer was never enough for him. To me, it was a simple matter of Grandma's life having run its course. Grandma Helen had run the race with faith and had now crossed the finish line.

How do you answer the question of why? I was annoyed, quite honestly, and as Rob and I drove back and forth to law school and the questions remained four years after her death, often I lost patience with his questions. Looking back now, I see my faith was small. It was untested and ungrounded. It was easy to chide Rob for lack of faith, but the truth is that he was facing the difficulty of having to choose to believe that which he could not see and that which he could not understand. This same decision is the most important question any of us will ever face.

~ ~ ~

I dream that Rob is playing football with his friends. I can't see who is playing receiver. Rob holds the football in his right hand, resting it briefly on his left palm, draws his throwing arm back, then suddenly glances over at me and cackles with laughter. When he cackled like that it was only because he knew whatever he had just said or done had irritated me.

He annoyed me because he loved me. And now that I'm older I understand that this is true. He annoyed me because he loved me.

But now in this dream I see that instead of throwing the football, as usual, this time he hangs his head, turns and walks away. He no longer had the gumption to tease me. I don't know exactly when the teasing stopped. I do know he made a halfhearted attempt the night before he died, when he palmed my pregnant belly and told me it was like holding a basketball. He looked up at me in an unusual way, almost as if he was chewing his fingernails in his mind, wondering how I would receive this.

Who was this Rob? I see now how much he had changed. For so much of my life, Rob was sure of himself, or at least sure of his direction. He was almost always chasing something. When Rob had a goal, it was as if the 99 percent faded around him and his field of vision was entirely consumed by the 1 percent that contained that goal.

The 1 percent changed over the years. For much of his life it was basketball until he hit college and realized he needed a backup plan.

We watched the movie "Rounders" together one evening, coincidentally along with my future husband before we started dating. "Rounders" is about a law student who plays high-stakes poker on the side. Rob was fixated on law school after this movie and promptly started the enrollment process. But soon after starting law school, we all knew it wasn't the best fit for Rob. He was intelligent and capable, but he wasn't reading or keeping up on assignments. It was clear by the end of his first semester that he was underperforming. He could have done better, but after two years, much heartburn, diagnosis of an anxiety disorder, and a prescription for anti-anxiety medication, he dropped out. He was one year short of his law degree.

He was married by this time, with a baby on the way. He felt pressure to buckle down, but was struggling to find his way. His next goal was a career as a fireman. But soon after training and then starting that job, again we knew it wasn't a great fit for Rob.

Firefighters face life and death situations and adrenaline often runs high. This was not an ideal environment for a tender spirit like

Rob. Once again, he was in a situation where he would feel anxious and out of place.

Rob was with the fire department for just a few months before he died. About a month before he took his life, he ran a call to a house fire and was involved in an extraordinary accident.

I received the call about the house fire as I sat in my law office typing at my computer. Once again, I twirled a phone cord around my finger as I received a memorable call. My dad was calling to let me know Rob had fallen through the floor of a burning house, but he was okay. He had landed on a mattress in the basement.

Rob's fall and soft landing on the mattress was such a miraculous event he was featured on a local news story that someone told my family even made national news outlets for a short cycle. Rob, never one lacking in flair, told the reporter he was feeling "a little discombobulated" but other than that he was fine.

We laughed that Rob would say "discombobulated" in a news interview, perhaps a historic first use of the word on the local television station, and we marveled that he was safe. What were the odds he would land on a mattress?

Rob didn't take it so lightly. The grace of God saved Rob from injury or death that day. But he was annoyed with the attention he received from his fall. Rob was annoyed with almost everyone and everything at that time in his life.

He said he was annoyed because it was such a waste of time to be here on Earth. Why did he have to be here when Grandma Helen was up in heaven having fun? This was seven years after her death, and he was still fixated on her departure at the age of twenty-seven. Grief is unique to each person, and uniquely expressed. He was fixated, almost to the point of obsession. And after the fall in the burning house, he began to withdraw from life. He wasn't sleeping well, and in time we would determine he was suffering from severe anxiety and depression.

Looking back, I see that Rob was exhibiting many warning signs of suicide: The lack of enthusiasm in things that he once enjoyed, the change in appearance, the increasing isolation, the combativeness, the deep questions about death.

I wish I had known more about the warning signs. I also wish I had known that someone like Rob, with so much talent and potential, was not immune to depression or thoughts of taking his life. I wish I had known how difficult it is to live with depression and that a person can't simply "snap out of it."

What I miss most about Rob was his questioning mind. He was a deep thinker. He thought through things thoroughly and with fervor. One evening our family dined together with a gentleman named Doug, my husband's new friend from medical school. Rob had never met Doug but instantly we knew Rob trusted him because he felt comfortable jumping right in with questions.

"Doug, can I ask you a really personal question?" Rob said within five minutes of introduction. We held our breath when Doug agreed, never knowing what might come out of Rob's mouth. "If you had to choose between Michael Jordan in his prime or Kobe Bryant in his prime in a game of one-on-one, who would you choose?" We let out a peal of laughter to hear what Rob considered to be "a really personal question."

We laughed at the time. Now I see that for all his quirks his innocence was a delight. Rob transcended conversation, even the very atmosphere around him, into another realm. He was supernaturally curious and his thoughts were not in the pattern of the world. He was a necessary antidote to the poison of conformity all around him, and yet it seemed he questioned whether the essence of who he was was good enough for the fact he couldn't conform.

Those who met Rob, even in passing, remember him. I spoke to a group about Rob a few years back. Afterward a woman in the audience approached to let me know she met Rob once about eight years earlier. She spent fifteen minutes with him, taking his blood pressure and other vitals as a part of Rob's job on the fire department. She said Rob looked her in the eye. He asked about her life, her kids, her grandkids, her job. I'm sure he smiled at her that way he always smiled, and I'm sure he was quiet and insightful like he could be. In that fifteen minutes, Rob made an unforgettable impression on her.

I could share Rob's story and without her even seeing a picture or hearing a last name, this woman knew instantly he was the young man who had been kind to her eight years earlier.

~ ~ ~

Rob loved basketball. I said that already, but I have more to tell you about his love of the game. In high school days before cell phones, when he met up with his buddies, we knew we could find him on the court playing basketball.

In summer, he and his best friend Jon played ball into the twilight at the basketball court in the Sibley park. Across the street was a place called the Park Store, where we bought Gatorade, candy bars and Big Grab bags of Doritos. I needed a ride home after hanging out with my friends and so I sat there, keeping watch over snacks half-eaten in their wrappers, while Rob and Jon shot hoops even after the lights turned on and the mosquitoes came out. Yes, it seems I told you this already. Forgive me for repeating myself. It's just that it takes me back to a moment when all seemed right in the world.

Rob somehow found a way to get inside the local VFW, which housed a small gym perfect for playing winter ball indoors. I stood outside the VFW numerous times pounding against the door, once again needing a ride home, but the guys were too engrossed in their game to hear the pounding and let me in. It was humorous. I could see Rob's car outside, and I could see a glimpse of his dark hair bobbing around inside every now and again as he ran back and forth on the court, and yet there I was stuck outside in the cold with no way to get in.

A dream some years later would remind me of those evenings standing in the snow and wind outside the VFW, knocking on the door to get Rob's attention. It was a dream about Rob that seems to illustrate perfectly the grief and despair I felt about his death and the hope in my heart for others struggling with depression.

~ ~ ~

In the dream, Rob was playing in a final championship basketball game, wearing his old, red mesh high school practice jersey neatly tucked into his basketball shorts.

The wooden gym floor gleamed a polished golden color. The scoreboard and clock were suspended from the center of the gym ceiling, visible to the crowd but not to the players on the court. The gym was encased in a Plexiglas® cube separating players from the spectators. The game was close. Rob played forward or point guard. I could never distinguish between those two positions. It was apparent from watching that the outcome of the game rested on Rob's shoulders. Rob dribbled upcourt and reached the top of the key. For the life of me, I cannot remember if he shot and missed or whether he passed to another player who shot and missed. All I know is the ball didn't go in the hoop.

As the shot bounced off the rim, the rest of the players faded into the background. I saw Rob turn around, walking back up the court, his shoulders falling forward in dejection. But I looked at the clock and saw there was still time remaining. It was only a few seconds. But the game wasn't over.

The clock was hanging above Rob where we could see it but he could not. He kept his head down and walked off the court. He didn't see me on the sidelines pointing up at the clock or hear me pounding on the Plexiglas.

I tried pounding louder and began screaming, but he did not hear me and did not look up. "Rob, don't quit!! There's still time on the clock! You can still win this thing!! YOU CAN STILL WIN!!!"

The Plexiglas was the problem. I beat on it with my fists, looked around for something to smash through it and started peeling away at it with my fingernails.

The first layer peeled away like a thin layer of string cheese, but I still wasn't breaking through for Rob to hear me. I pressed harder. Desperation mounted. My hands were starting to hurt. I looked down to see blood on my hands and shards of the Plexiglas wedged under my nails. A weight of despondency washed over me. I knew there was nothing else I could do.

At that moment, the buzzer sounded and the game really was over.

Rob never knew. He never knew enough time remained for him to win. Everyone else could see it, but he could not.

I awoke in sobs, still desperate to reach Rob. My desperation turned to sadness as I realized again that he was gone.

No matter what I dream about Rob, every morning I wake up to the reality he is dead. I am sorry to have to tell you that Rob did not look up at the crowd, that I could not break through the Plexiglas, that I did not have the right tools with me, that my hands were bleeding and I was screaming so loud it hurt my lungs. I am so sorry to have to tell you that the buzzer sounded and the game is over for Rob.

And yet for some reason, the more I stew over this dream, the more it brings me immense comfort. Even as I write about it, my fingers trip over themselves with alacrity as I recall with conviction that even in the darkness of Rob's death, a promise is written therein for the rest of us.

The symbolism wrapped up in that dream seems to reflect that Rob was laboring under an incorrect belief. Everyone around Rob could see the clock and knew that time remained. We all knew Rob could have won the game handily. But he could not see it for himself, a reality so true of the depressed mind.

A seemingly impenetrable wall separated us from Rob, but with the right tools that wall would have come down. Even a simple tool, as simple as an axe, would have done a mighty work in that moment of despair. I think of how my mom and I used to scratch Rob's scalp as he stretched out on the pew in evening church. If only I could walk by him one more time and give his scalp a gentle and playful scratch, to feel his coarse dark hair in my fingers, to send him the sisterly signal to remind him of when we were little kids and to say without words "thank you for watching over me so well" and to say without words "I still love you now like I loved you then." He would have known

what I meant, and even though a simple act, it might have broken through that wall.

I feel a burning in my heart as I share this dream. Can you feel, as you read it, the intensity of how incorrect the entire situation was? How not true Rob's belief was? Can you place yourself in the crowd alongside me, watching Rob walk off the basketball court with time left on the clock? What would you have done? For those of us who struggle with anxiety or depression or hopelessness, can you picture yourself on the basketball court? Are you willing to look at the crowd, to look up at the clock and to let the truth penetrate your mind and spirit?

There is always time on the clock for us. No matter how many bad passes we make or how many shots roll out of the hoop or even how many air balls we fling, there is always time on the clock for us. Our clock runs out of time when the Lord says, and not a moment before.

The Learning Years

About ten months after Rob died, my husband, our two girls and I moved to Harrisburg, Pennsylvania, for my husband's job. I told you this already, too. There is more to share about this time in our lives. We moved across the country, arriving Memorial Day weekend of 2006, knowing only one person on the entire Eastern seaboard.

I always imagined I might live somewhere farther east than our farm in Iowa. I just never expected "living out East" would involve a full graduate school course load, two young children, no local support system and a husband who worked 80 to 100 hours a week.

Pretty quickly after we moved, it hit me that my life was growing progressively worse. This took me by surprise. I guess I'd always figured life was supposed to get better. There might be a hiccup or two, one or two tragedies maximum, but life overall would continue to become…well, better than before.

There's this passage in the book of Lamentations that seemed fitting at the time:

> *He has broken my teeth with gravel. He has trampled me in the dust. I have been deprived of peace. I have forgotten what prosperity is. So I say, My splendor is gone and all that I had hoped from the Lord. I remember my affliction and my wandering, the bitterness and the gall. I well remember them, and my soul is downcast within me.*

Lamentations 3:16-20.

This segment from Lamentations is a very depressing passage, and yet for some reason, reading it in the years after Rob died made me feel less alone.

I wondered if the writer knew what it was like to have gravel in his mouth, literally, and I felt kinship with him. Our driveway back on the farm in Iowa was covered in gravel. One day as curious little kids, Rob and I tried to chew a handful of this gravel. It leaves a strange taste and texture. It dries out the mouth and makes a person thirsty. Yet when you take a drink, it seems to reformulate the dust inside the mouth into a thick coating of mud. It was always quite unpleasant.

I understood the writer in other ways, too. It seemed what I was going through was the morale equivalent of everything he wrote. Not moral. Morale. My morale was destroyed.

Looking back, I see my life was in a deconstruction phase. Feeble walls were torn down. Crumbling foundations were ripped up. While at the time it seemed I was losing—going backwards. I now see that the removal process was making way for the rebuilding.

~ ~ ~

I never pictured myself as a tax attorney. After all, I didn't wear a pocket protector and I was horrible at keeping track of documents and receipts, those sorts of things.

In law school, the day of our federal income taxation final, I was sick with strep throat, had studied very little and yet managed to earn a 96, one point away from the high grade in the course. A professor of mine, a sort-of mentor who taught a subject not really related to taxation at all, somehow knew about my grade in the course and suggested I pursue this as an advanced area of study. I had no interest at that point in time.

However, as months and years passed, I thought more about taxation, wondering if I should—and ultimately deciding I wanted to—pursue it as a career. The problem was that the closest school to Sioux Falls, where I lived, offering an advanced law degree in taxation was over four hours away.

But when we moved to Pennsylvania and as I struggled to find a job that would accommodate our busy lives, I began looking into it. I settled on a program less than two hours away in the upscale Philadelphia-area Main Line suburbs. I began in the fall of 2006, setting out at 4 p.m. on the Pennsylvania Turnpike, I-76, in order to make the 6 p.m. class, and returning home around midnight, several nights a week.

During the day, I was busy with our two young girls; the oldest not yet 5 and our youngest 9 months old. The schedule was grueling, what with rising at 7 a.m. with the baby after falling asleep at 1 or 2 a.m. the night before after the drive home from school.

I started suffering from anxiety and depression that fall. Several times I was unable to make the drive down to Philadelphia because of panic attacks on the turnpike.

You see, there was a cement barrier on the turnpike between the opposing lanes of traffic, and one day as I drove on the inside lane near the cement barrier, a truck passed me on my right I knew in that moment I was going to die. I was convinced of it. The truck next to me was in fact at a safe distance, yet I knew that this was all a mirage and that the truth was that it was going to drift into my lane to crush me and my vehicle between it and the cement barrier. In the face of this impending disaster, I had no choice but to stop breathing, yet I knew I should try to breathe, so I took in a huge gulp of air, and the confusion in my lungs and in my body caused my vision to momentarily blacken. I was panicking. Convinced I had escaped death and so as not to tempt fate any further, I turned around at the next exit to return home. This was a recurring thing that started happening. I knew it wasn't real, yet it felt so real and I didn't know how to make the thoughts stop.

There were also the afternoons and evenings when I felt bold and brave, resolving to attend the later 8 p.m. class, intending to leave town at 6 p.m. for the two-hour drive. But many of these evenings, I drove my kids downtown to the hospital to drop them off where my husband worked, only to wait with them in the hospital lobby for fifteen minutes, then thirty minutes, until finally the hands on the clock approached 7 p.m. and my husband was still in surgery. And so I missed those classes, too.

As finals approached, I was behind on my studies, which, honestly, wasn't unusual for me as I tended to procrastinate. And yet there was more material here than with any other courses I'd ever taken. I was exhausted. Several times I resolved to drop out of the program entirely, yet an internal check stopped me from doing so.

One evening, a few days before finals, I sat at the kitchen counter with my head in my hands. "I can't do this," I thought. "Lord, help me. I can't do this on my own." It occurred to me that for perhaps one of the first times in my life, I might not succeed. I might not be able to do it on my own.

A restfulness settled over me, knowing that perhaps I couldn't do it, but also knowing that all I needed to do was to try and that the results were in the hands of a higher power.

I stayed in the program and took the finals. The day grades were released, I traveled to Philadelphia to discuss a registration matter with the head of the tax program. I recall walking into the trailer where the Graduate Tax Program office was housed temporarily during a construction project and seeing the friendly face of the program coordinator. I wore my long, black wool coat with fur trim, and remember feeling exceptionally tall.

She asked how I had done in my classes. I gushed to her that my final grades were just released and that I had earned an "A" in each of my five classes. I was flabbergasted. I shared how I had almost dropped out and how I suffered from panic attacks on the way down to class some evenings. I was simply stunned at the result after such a difficult semester.

She was stunned, too. I recall her saying, "Mary, that doesn't happen," and that only a few previous students had earned all A's when taking those five classes together. She suggested I apply for an internship with the Internal Revenue Service. Working in government was a deep-seated interest since childhood. I earned a spot in the summer internship program, delighted at the chance to work in Center City Philadelphia for a summer. I had come a long way from spraying weeds in an Iowa bean field on a farm ten miles from the nearest town.

Still, I wasn't sure it was going to work, juggling babysitters and my husband's work schedule. I would have to leave Harrisburg at 4 a.m. to drive to Philadelphia in time to catch the R5 commuter train to arrive in Center City around 7:30 a.m.

My mind was busy on the practicalities of the decision. My mom saw the gift in the opportunity. She encouraged me to think beyond the daily grind to see the long-term value so often gained through short-term pain. She was right. This opportunity was a gift. I took a leap of faith and committed to the internship.

On my first day of work, I was half an hour ahead of schedule, relaxed and ready to rumble. Looking smart in my black wool pantsuit, naïve to Philadelphia's hot and sticky summer climate, I strode into the train station restroom to freshen up after the train ride. I walked into the restroom, which was empty except for a homeless woman bending over washing her hair in the sink.

It occurred to me I had never encountered someone who so openly allowed others to see the reality of their need.

It occurred to me my commute and the hassles of the internship were in fact a luxury: I had a shower in my house, a closet of clean clothes, a car to drive and cash to pay for the train ride. I had so much, but was surrounded by others who also had so much that it took the jarring sight of a woman willing to wash her hair in a dirty, forsaken train station bathroom to gain perspective.

I emerged from the underground train station and hit the pavement in search of the IRS office. I have never since sweat so much in a black suit as I did that morning. I wandered the streets of the City of Brotherly Love, lost and looking for a well-hidden IRS office to no avail, finally running the sidewalks of the city in three-inch heels until I found the right building. My makeup was smeared, my confidence was shot and my nerves were worn down by the time I finally found the internship office, with not a minute to spare on that first morning.

At the end of the day, I took the R5 train back to the station where I had parked that morning. By this time, the sun was beating down so intensely that waves of heat radiated off the asphalt.

I walked over to my silver Jeep, at the far end of the parking lot, and saw a gentleman a few paces alongside me walking over to his Acura. I tried the key, but my Jeep wouldn't start. Again and again, I turned the key, to no avail. I flagged down the gentleman in the Acura before he drove off. He kindly tried to jump my car, but again, no response. I called AAA, thank goodness, and when the man arrived in his tow truck, I was certain my nightmare of a day had ended. He tried jumping it, but it still didn't start. He crawled under the car, tried something else unsuccessfully, then stood up and looked at me. I knew without a word spoken that I might be stuck in Philly for the night, in which case my kids would be home alone unless my babysitter was willing to spend the night while my husband took call at the hospital.

The AAA mechanic told me he had tried everything technical and then said, if it was okay with me, he would try one last thing. You can imagine how I prayed. He pulled a sledgehammer from his tow truck and said that on the count of three I was to turn the key. I don't know what he pounded or how it worked. But the car started, with a clang of the sledge hammer under the Jeep and a final turn of the key. "Don't turn off the car until you get home," he warned, "or you will be stuck wherever you turn it off." I remember running into a restroom off the turnpike, my Jeep sitting in the parking lot, engine running and doors unlocked.

The next morning I returned to the internship, feeling overwhelmed, wondering through tears why all this was happening to me. I had taken a leap of faith, knowing the internship would not be easy. Why was God not smoothing out the bumps for me?

At lunch, alone, I walked around the block, discovering an underground tunnel from the train station to the IRS building. The tunnel was lined with kiosks selling cheap sunglasses, scarves, and handmade inspirational signs and gifts.

One inspirational sign said, "Faith Doesn't Make Things Easy. It Makes Things Possible."

I stopped in my tracks, overwhelmed with emotion as I gazed at the sign. In that moment, I recognized I understood very little of what faith requires in the daily struggles of life. Improper expectations were uprooted, and I began to understand what I should expect when I step out in faith. Circumstances may not be easy. In fact, I would venture to say that rarely is it easy stepping out in faith.

Yet anything is possible.

~ ~ ~

With my resume freshly padded with a Master of Laws in Taxation and an IRS internship, I found work at a governmental agency a few miles from our home in Harrisburg. It was a great relief to find something so close to home offering a family-friendly career option.

The agency's offices were located in Strawberry Square, a sixteen-story building in the center of the capital city of the sixth most populous state in the nation. It offered a prime view of the Pennsylvania capitol building, replete with a food court, escalator, and whimsical chiming clock.

If Mary Tyler Moore were to live in Harrisburg, she too would have wanted to work in Strawberry Square, where people milled about, taking a rest as they awaited a meeting or a legislative vote, or stopping for a moment on their way from the train station to the capitol. We even had a Starbucks.

My first day of work was a cold February day. That blustery morning I parked in the wrong parking garage. I traveled to the wrong floor and entered the wrong set of offices where I explained breathlessly that I was a new lawyer there for my first day of work. The discreet receptionist informed me, kindly, that the Chief Counsel's Office, where I was headed, was on the tenth floor just below, and that this was the eleventh floor, the executive suite. I would later learn the eleventh floor was the important floor where one is supposed to speak in hushed tones. My cheeks blush even thinking about that morning.

It was a morning of many foibles, in some ways similar to the first morning of the IRS internship, but this go-round was easier to overcome. The IRS internship had seasoned me, teaching me to persist and to keep my head up even when I hit bumps in the road.

Aside from those first-morning foibles, the start of my career at Strawberry Square was a golden moment, a time of excitement and revelation and self-discovery. It was an enthusiasm you want to hold in your hands but can't, because you can't contain that sort of thing.

I felt as if I might learn things I could not learn elsewhere. I would meet people, exciting people, and witness exciting moments that would alter the rest of my life. I felt like a kid again.

But it was also a stressful time, with a husband working long days, often around the clock, for his surgical residency, and me feeling as if I was raising two young children on my own while working full-time.

The days passed quickly and began to run together. I had hoped for excitement and revelation and self-discovery. Instead, I felt like a hamster on a wheel. The days became a drill; alarm, shower, kids to daycare, work, return home to make dinner and bathe the kids, only to start the same routine all over again the next morning.

I didn't recognize it at the time, but in those mundane months and years I see now that in fact I *was* in the midst of excitement and revelation and self-discovery, but only in a way observable in the rear-view mirror.

In those months and years working at the agency, I met two gentlemen whose lives taught me a whole lot about myself and the world around me.

The first of the two gentleman was Secretary 1, the head of our agency. I arrived about the same time as he did, and would soon learn his reputation and credentials were sterling. I imagined he was quite possibly a descendant of a Knight of the Round Table.

We saw him from a distance periodically near the agency elevators, our group of young attorneys eyeing him discreetly. I sat in on a meeting with him one of my first weeks at the agency. Nervous out of my mind, nervous down to my knees, I grabbed a seat in a black leather chair at the conference table in the executive meeting room. It seemed from our limited encounter that the secretary was a sage man able to conduct meetings with maximum efficiency without rushing the process in any way.

This man would be elected Governor of Pennsylvania several years later.

The recession hit in 2008, and Secretary 1 stepped down to return to his family's business, which was struggling along with the national economy. In his place, another secretary was named, this time a congenial gentleman with a vibrant, energetic air about him. We will call him Secretary 2.

The two secretaries were so different, yet each was effective.

Secretary 2 was effective because he could read a room and because the people in the room instantly knew he liked them. He was someone you could drop off in the middle of a desert with a bottle of water and a compass, and who would show up at home ten days later sharing stories of all the incredible people who helped him find his way.

The secretary's office was on the eleventh floor, the executive floor I inadvertently visited that first morning, just above our Chief Counsel's Office. Our office's law library looked onto a hallway with a door to the stairwell connecting the two floors. I stood in the library one day reading out of a musty, leather bound book. I looked up and saw Secretary 2 walking to the stairwell along with a cadre of other high-level executives from the agency.

He glanced into the library for a brief second and smiled kindly at me. I recall thinking his hair looked longer than usual, unkempt and inconsistent with his usual impressive appearance. It also seemed, though I can't pinpoint why, that he seemed off his game, not the confident leader we knew.

A few hours later, we would all learn he had just resigned and was soon to be indicted in "Bonusgate," a criminal investigation into activities in the state legislature.

I cried when I heard the news. I cried at my desk, with my door shut, head down in my hands in disbelief, and cried on the car ride home and again that evening at home while making dinner. I cried after washing my face for the evening, and had to wash my face all over again to remove the salty tears caked on my face.

I cried because from what I observed and what I heard said of him, this was a good man. A good man who, in spite of what allegedly may have happened years ago, was now undoubtedly wiser. He executed his duties with kindness and sensitivity. He brought color and life to our hamster-wheel governmental agency lives. And now we would no longer have him in our midst.

From what is publicly available, Secretary 2 was part of a group of legislators who, years before, had allegedly used staff members to conduct campaign activities. They were charged with improperly commingling legislative and campaign activities. He was convicted and sentenced to prison.

We could have all sorts of discussions about the legal and penal system, whether restitution and community service would have been a more appropriate punishment. We could debate the motives of the prosecution. We could talk extensively about Pennsylvania politics, all of the investigations, insinuations and infighting that puts the beloved foundational state of our union in a league of its own. Yet the fact remains that the secretary went to prison and I believe this was not the right result.

What burdened me most for Secretary 2 that day is I wanted to protect him from any labels that people may put on him. I knew people might someday attach labels such as "prisoner" or perhaps even "felon" when they spoke of him, and I felt powerless to prevent this. "He is a good man so do not say these things!" I wanted to yell from the rooftops.

I realize now this is because of Rob. Many who die by suicide are labeled.

People ask me if I have any siblings. "I had only a brother, but he is gone," I say. They are sorry to hear that. They ask me what happened. "He died by suicide," I say. They feel bad for asking. They do not know what to say. They are so kind to ask. I am thankful they care.

I know you care, too. The kindest thing you can do is to avoid labels. It is a simple restraint of mercy on those who suffer. Mine the gold in the lives of those around you, whether dead or alive, and discard the dross.

Please, don't label Rob or others in chains of any kind, whether depression or addiction or in literal prison chains because of acts no longer reflecting the actor.

Rob was so good to me. He wasn't crazy or a quitter or whatever people might think when they hear of someone who died by suicide. He was my brother, and I loved him.

~ ~ ~

My dad is around the same age as the two gentlemen who served as secretary. And like one of them, he too was in chains at one point in his life, only his were chains of grief.

As a little girl, he picked me up from preschool or half-day kindergarten and I sat on the center armrest in the front seat of my dad's car, chattering away as we drove the forty-five minutes to Sioux Falls, South Dakota, the nearby big city in our little corner of the world.

One afternoon on our way to Sioux Falls, he first explained to me the story of a man named Hitler and the slaughter of millions of innocent people who I later would learn were the European Jews.

I was in kindergarten. It was a heavy topic for our ride home, but a moment of awakening. For the first time, it seemed, I was entrusted with adult information giving insight into a world beyond me.

Before we moved to the farm, we lived in a home on the outskirts of the small northwest Iowa town next to a cornfield. Rob and I explored the cornfield one day, walking far down the shadowy rows of full-grown stalks. We reached a point of no return, knowing we were closer to the other side than we were to our home. I felt a moment of panic until we saw a glimpse of the other side of that field. There, much to our delight, we discovered a church yard with an enormous playground. It's interesting, those moments when it sets in that there is a world beyond one's backyard.

That day in the car, learning about Hitler, was the first time I understood that in the world beyond that cornfield or our little town or even the big city nearby there isn't always a playground on the other side.

I learned those things from my dad, and other important life skills such as how to fix a vacuum cleaner, how to clean a sprayer nozzle and how to check the oil on a tractor.

And then, twenty years later, there were days after Rob died when my dad was so angry his face grew purple with rage. I wouldn't even look him in the eye. His eyes had become threatening and dark. He was utterly destroyed after Rob died and it was evident for all to see.

We had moved to Pennsylvania by that time. Whenever my dad visited, stress and tumult were inevitable, to the point I couldn't bear him anymore. I suffered too much under the weight of my own internal stress and chaos.

"I don't think my dad is ever going to change. I don't want to speak to him anymore," I declared to my husband. I remember the statement, the conviction I felt as I declared this, as if I were saying it right now.

Looking back, I also recognize a release of some sort happened in me. It was as if I let go of my dad. I let go of resentment. I let go of judgment. I let go of worry or control.

And so, for awhile, I stopped speaking to my dad.

My dad was diagnosed with skin and prostate cancer within less than a year, and in those moments facing his own death, he responded to the call to reconcile himself to God. He started seeing a counselor at the urging of my mom. In that process, my dad worked through the anger and fears and regrets he felt from Rob's death, and returned not only to the man he used to be, but, beyond that, to a better version of the man he used to be. Ironically, it was my dad from whom I would learn how to start the healing process.

I can't pinpoint when I knew he had changed. I do recall, however, sitting at a table with him at Houlihan's, a restaurant in Hershey, Pennsylvania, a few miles from our home. We were enjoying an appetizer sampler and mini desserts, sitting across the table from one other, and it occurred to me my dad and I were sitting together and there was peace. Possibly even joy.

These several years later, my husband and I still remark that my dad is one of the happiest people we know, released from his pain and now free to reflect, well, the joy of freedom.

People absolutely can change. There is always hope for them.

~ ~ ~

I could see the change in my dad, and knew it was possible to break free of grief. Yet I didn't see a counselor right away. Something inside me believed I would return to my normal self after we moved closer to family and friends in the Midwest. And so I waited, looking forward to the day conditions would change.

June 18, 2011, our three girls and I moved back to Sioux Falls, South Dakota, near family and our old friends. My husband moved to Iowa City, Iowa, where he was to complete a one-year surgical fellowship. He commuted back and forth to Sioux Falls on weekends and holidays.

Over a year before moving back to Sioux Falls, I nailed down a position at a law firm in town. In law school, I had interned at this firm, awestruck watching brilliant lawyers in action. I wanted more than anything to be a part of their team. It became a career goal. A goal to work at that law firm.

Eight years after my internship, I walked up to the front door of that law firm in a black skirt suit and heels, prepared to feel satisfaction at having accomplished a career goal. Except I didn't feel satisfied. In fact, the thought I had as I crossed the threshold of the front door was, "I do not want to be here." That thought—"I do not want to be here"—had nothing to do with the law firm. It had everything to do with me. I had changed. Everything I once held dear now held no meaning for me.

I did go to work there, but as the days began to wear on, the thought would resurface again and again. "I do not want to be here." I had changed.

This gradual awakening grieved me tremendously. I had always known what I wanted. I had always wanted to work at that law firm. Yet with the job finally in hand after years of thinking about it, here came the emptiness alongside.

I felt unanchored, drifting. It was as if I had taken a journey in a flimsy rowboat, paddling toward coordinates of an island on a map, relentlessly and singularly seeking it as a place to anchor, only to reach the coordinates and find the island wasn't there. All that energy, all that hope, suddenly I discovered to be futile.

Every dream was fulfilled and none of it had satisfied. I had nothing to look forward to anymore. I was tired, weary to the very bone. How could I think God had a future for me in the midst of all that?

~ ~ ~

When you have a career path and you reach what you thought was the goal and find that it wasn't, what happens next?

I stood at the doorway to the next chapter of life with no idea what was beyond. And so I started to think, "What do I really want out of life? And what will it take for me to pursue it?"

In December of 2012, I noticed a strange mole on my stomach.

Around the same time, my husband and I attended a Christmas party with his future co-workers and their spouses. At the party, I got the distinct impression from the co-workers' wives that their lives were still hectic. Life wasn't slowing down much after all those years of training. For years, the idea of a more tranquil life had kept me afloat. I could juggle work and the rest of life because I believed someday my husband would be able to alleviate a portion of that burden. This Christmas party was telling me all these hopes were a mirage. A few days after that Christmas party, I awoke in the night gasping for air, sobbing without tears. In a dream, I had been dying of cancer. The spot on my stomach was deadly melanoma.

In my dream, I was trying to speak. Trying to explain to someone all the things I'd always wanted to do with my girls before I died. It was too soon. I hadn't yet had time to waste watching TV with them in the summertime, candy wrappers and bags of chips scattered all around us just like Rob and I used to do when we were kids and our mom wasn't home. I hadn't yet had time to take them to the pool on hot days, so that they might have the experience I always envied other kids for when I was their age. I hadn't yet had the chance to be home with them when they were sick, without worrying about sick days or the unanswered email. I hadn't yet had time to invest deeply in developing their faith and their character. I hadn't had time to be available. I awoke and started crying. My husband was in Iowa City.

Our youngest daughter, just a few months old, slept in the crib in our room. I slipped into my closet, turning on the light and shutting the door, sobbing out loud, my chest heaving as I thought about this dream.

I told you—when I walked through the door of the law firm and realized I didn't want to be there—it seemed everything had been taken from me. That I had nothing to aspire to. That even desire was gone.

This dream told me this was not true. I had a desire. A desire to be free of it all. After years of stress, juggling our two careers, racing to day care, hurrying the kids to bed so I might keep working after they fell asleep, after all that, all I wanted was to have time to spend with my kids.

The only thing that stood in my way was me. "Who am I if I am not a lawyer?" I wondered.

I considered working at a nonprofit or working part time or volunteering for political campaigns. As I stripped away the layers and discarded the options coursing through my mind, it occurred to me I might stay home. This finally was a viable option by that point in time, an incredible gift there for the taking.

But what was I if not a lawyer?

It's a truism about getting so wrapped up in finding our identity through jobs or activities or appearance that sometimes it's difficult to disentangle ourselves and to find our real selves under all that stuff on the surface. Was I proving the truism to be valid?

The blessings in life, such as our education, can sometimes become a noose around our neck, choking us and holding us hostage. So many people told me it was foolish to throw away all my years of study and training, to throw away a good job. You'll regret your decision, they all seemed to say.

I don't answer to them.

The Bible says if you trust in the Lord with all your heart, He will give you the desires of your heart. What did I desire? I desired to stop taking out the stress of work on my children. I desired to lie by them in bed on sick days without feeling anger vacillating to panic to fear at the thought of being away from the office. I desired not to have to act serious all the time, to be silly and free and creative without watching the clock. I desired to be able to stop thinking "what if?"

Once I knew what I wanted, it only took the courage to stand up and walk away.

The mole on my stomach turned out to be fine.

I left the law firm a few months later so I could stay home with my kids.

It was painful. It scared me to walk away. It scared me to see how many layers had to be stripped until I was willing to let go of the person I thought I had to be.

I see now that in letting go, I was making space to become the person I was meant to be. There really was a future, but first, I would have to let go of the past and the pressures of who I thought I had to be.

~ ~ ~

After leaving my job, I struggled with increasingly debilitating anxiety and depression. Only after leaving my job I was without an excuse. I no longer worked outside the home. I lived near family. My family—my husband and children—were doing well. On the surface, I had no justifiable reason for struggling.

It sounds simple now, writing about these painful years in a few sentences. I've often wondered how a person might make a movie about depression and anxiety that is accurate yet one people might actually sit through for two hours. It's like this: Life consists of an endless reel of negative and hopeless thoughts. You replay all the ways you screwed up that day. You worry about everything that can go wrong, like the moment of dread before answering the phone, fearing without reason that the person on the other end of the line is going to yell at you. You sense hope and excitement for a moment, thinking breakthrough may be near, but then a careless word or glance from a loved one punctures the thin skin starting to form over the deep wounds, leaving raw, exposed emotion in its stead. In those moments when wounds are reopened, the glimmer of excitement is extinguished, as if by a bucket of cold water thrown on the smallest spark.

All those years, people told me they admired me. In their eyes, I was educated, accomplished and well-married. I possessed every-thing they thought they wanted.

I longed to tell them the truth, but believed the truth would dis-appoint them. I couldn't bear to tell them that a dream job won't bring you happiness. That a marriage to a lovely husband won't bring you happiness. That healthy, vibrant children won't bring you happiness. Because what hope do we have if everything that everyone aspires to doesn't bring happiness? What is left in life? The weight of the lies weighed on my conscience. I couldn't bear to live a lie any longer.

I started to open up about my struggles and disappointments. In doing so, an interesting thing happened. Friends started opening up to me about their struggles. Friends from long ago, as far back as middle school, started contacting me on Facebook to tell me about their struggles, that they had nowhere to turn and were desperately looking for rest from their weariness. One of these friends thanked me for helping her along. As we talked about the course of our lives, I confessed how hard it had been to talk about my struggles openly.

"I worried people would think I was weak," I said.

Her response to this caught me off-guard.

"I don't think people perceived you as weak when you shared those things. I think they perceived you as real."

Real. This struck me. It struck me because, as soon as she said it, it occurred to me I had really wanted her to tell me I was perceived as strong. I wanted people to think I was strong, but instead they thought I was real.

I've thought about this quite a bit since. I wanted to be strong so people might admire me and perhaps even revere me. But that wasn't what they needed. They needed to know they aren't alone in their struggles. It's funny. I think we all have the desire to encourage and lift others up. After years of trying, I discovered our greatest resource is not in projecting an image of strength and perfection–that only serves to intimidate others–but rather, through sharing stories of the reality behind that image.

The Start of Healing

> *God is light. In Him there is no darkness at all. If we claim to have fellowship with him and yet walk in the darkness, we lie and do not live out the truth. But if we walk in the light, as he is in the light, we have fellowship with one another, and the blood of Jesus, his Son, purifies us from all sin.*

> *If we claim to be without sin, we deceive ourselves and the*
> *truth is not in us. If we confess our sins, he is faithful and*
> *just and will forgive us our sins and purify us from all un-*
> *righteousness.*

1 John 1:5-9.

Sometimes you hear stories of miraculous, instantaneous heal-ings. I do believe those happen. More often, though, healing arrives through a series of small events. Those events appear unrelated until later you look back and see how, when woven together, they've worked a miracle.

A spunky grandma in our church in Sioux Falls left me a voicemail after I quit my job at the law firm, inviting me to a Bible study called *Breaking Free*. Beth Moore wrote the study to cover a range of hindrances holding us back from a life of freedom.

This spunky grandma saw me at church a few days later. She grabbed my hand and invited me again.

I was willing to try the Bible study. I really was. But I was so anx-ious that I hated leaving the house. I was struggling with depression. I didn't want to feign happiness or an interest in others. The spunky grandma was persistent, though, and so I forced myself to go.

The Bible calls itself the word of God and tells us it is active and living, sharper than any two-edged sword. It is a God-breathed book, written by individuals appointed by God under the direction and influence of the Holy Spirit. And so when we read it, we are guided and prompted by the author, God himself.

A few weeks into the study we delved into those areas in our lives that might be hindering us from freedom. We were instructed to read a passage from the Old Testament book of Jeremiah. The pas-sage struck me to my core, so much so that I wrote in the margin the exact time and date at which I read it: January 27, 2013, 4:53 pm. This passage reads:

> *Hear and pay attention, do not be arrogant, for the Lord*
> *has spoken. Give glory to the Lord your God before he*
> *brings the darkness, before your feet stumble on the dark-*
> *ening hills. You hope for light, but he will turn it to thick*
> *darkness and change it to deep gloom. But if you do not*
> *listen, I will weep in secret because of your pride. My eyes*

> will weep bitterly, overflowing with tears, because the
> Lord's flock will be taken captive.

Jeremiah 13:15-17.

Pride, darkness and gloom. The words on the page were flashing neon lights. In a moment, it made sense. Pride was behind so much of my depression and sadness stemming from Rob's death. I was proud of my grief. My wounds were badges of honor. I relished the misery of Rob's death, claiming it as a mark that set me apart as a victim grievously harmed by God.

"The Lord owes me something."

A voice whispered it.

"The Lord has injured me beyond repair."

"If this is your plan for my life, Lord, I don't want it."

The lies and defiant thoughts kept coming.

After eight years the lies were a fixture of my subconscious. The lies are partial truths. Rob is gone. Death is final. We were wounded. But they weren't the whole truth. What of eternal life? And what of the power of the Holy Spirit to transform and heal us?

The Beth Moore study asked readers to consider whether lack of faith might be holding them back.

I almost skipped this entire section of the booklet. If you knew my spiritual pedigree you might have done the same. My Grandma Leta read through the Bible at least once a year. My Grandma Helen taught Bible school and evangelized the neighbor kids. My mom sat on our farmhouse porch for hours in prayer, reading her Bible or books by Christian authors. My aunt studied in Switzerland at L'Abri under Francis Schaeffer, the Christian theologian and philosopher. She was asked to stay on as his wife's personal assistant, choosing instead to return to the Midwest where she devoted her life to teaching in the public school system. And me? No sweat. I accepted Jesus in my heart at age 4 at the Okoboji Lakes Bible Conference. I memorized John 3:16 before I even started Awana Cubbies. And before I was in kindergarten, I stood in front of church at Easter and recited Psalm 23 in an excessively ruffled pink dress.

How could a believer like me, with such a heritage of faith, suffer from lack of faith? Still, a thought flashed through my mind: Don't dismiss this question.

I began to ask myself whether I believed there was hope I might be healed of my grief. After all, I had struggled with grief-induced anxiety and depression for almost eight years, and as a result, had wasted precious years of my life. Years in my prime, gone.

It dawned on me I did not believe I could be healed. Let me re-state that: I did not believe I could be healed. I felt nothing inside of me even close to belief. After eight years, it made no sense that things might ever improve. Did I believe it, and did I even want it?

And yet something told me I didn't need to feel the belief, like rainbows and butterflies, but that I only needed to humble myself to consider healing was possible. A mustard seed of faith.

I sat in the velvety gray recliner in our living room. I don't recall if I put the recliner's footrest down or just hopped out of the side of the chair or if the blanket over my legs got tangled up. I do remember that in one moment I was sitting in the recliner and in the next I was lowering to my knees on the plush cream-colored rug in our living room.

In that moment, I realized my prayers had been too small. I had put limitations on God, believing too little of Him and holding on to my resentment. I was in a standoff that I would never win. That day, I made the decision to turn over my grief to the Lord.

Once I opened the door to let Him into that area of my life, the Lord began to accelerate the healing process. Stuff started happening. Seemingly random, insignificant instances like the day a longtime friend called, encouraging me to see a counselor. She said to me, "You are not living up to your potential." And I cried. "Are you will-ing to do this to set a good example for your daughters?" she asked. And I cried harder.

This made sense, suddenly. I had long thought about seeing a counselor and had visited one a few times for sessions that I don't think helped me at all. I worked up the courage to talk to my physi-cian, who offered to prescribe me medication. I resisted only because I thought I needed to talk this all out first.

I visited a new counselor and, with that counselor, also found a friend. Not a friend exactly, but someone who could help me. We started meeting in the middle of a dark stretch of winter. I can still feel the shivers of fear as I sat in her office for the first time. It was terrifying to bare my soul. I couldn't even look her in the eye at times.

I felt pitiful that first day in her office, like I was weak and overly-dramatic to feel how I felt and to think what I thought so many years after Rob died. People lose loved ones all the time. What was my problem?

My problem was that the fears and the lies had taken up residence in my mind. The fears and the lies were such firmly entrenched patterns of thinking that it would require professional care and diligent effort on my part to develop new patterns of thinking. The flesh, those neural pathways in my brain, needed to be crucified.

Crucifying thoughts is as uncomfortable as it sounds. Talking about pain in order to develop new pathways of thinking about pain literally is painful. Before an appointment, sometimes even days before an appointment, sharp pains shot through my neck. My head and back ached. After the appointments, I felt flayed open. I was irritable and unsettled, often suffering from loss of sleep for a few nights after. I wanted to quit seeing the counselor. But I kept going.

In spite of the pain, within a few weeks of appointments, I discovered I was returning to the girl I used to be. I knew I was healing when I had a strong desire to go to a high school basketball game. Basketball games were a highlight of my youth, but for years after Rob died, the thought of attending a basketball game shot waves of panic right through me. After a few weeks of counseling, inexplicably, I wanted to go to a basketball game.

After a few weeks of counseling, I looked forward to seeing people again. I didn't fear having to put on a good front, because the front matched the interior. The smile was real again.

Holy Spirit

Even as healing occurred through counseling, the Lord was revealing new depths and means of healing.

It came in a time of extreme stress, when on all sides I felt suffocated by difficult circumstances. Through a curious twist of circumstances, I found myself again in a stressful situation inducing panic attacks and severe anxiety.

My mom knew what I faced, and so she invited me to visit the local prayer center where she volunteered. She thought it might help me reach peace and resolution over this situation. I wasn't so sure. After all, couldn't I just pray about it at home?

The prayer center was a non-denominational, nondescript setup in an office downtown with a staff of volunteers who prayed for people who walked in. My first visit was in April of 2014. Two women sat with me and listened as I poured out my worries.

As we started to pray together, one woman said, "Heavenly Father, we ask that the Holy Spirit speak to us while we pray."

Until that time, the Holy Spirit was, to me, the third wheel of the trinity. We all know God the Father and Jesus the Son, but it seems the Holy Spirit, our comforter and counselor dwelling in us after salvation, often is forgotten. For all I've read about the Holy Spirit, I'd never known we could actually have thoughts in our minds from God on an everyday, moment-by-moment basis to quench lies and to launch our thoughts to a higher plane of understanding.

As soon as the volunteer invited the Holy Spirit to speak to us as we prayed, instantly, all was quiet in my mind. All the chatter, the to-do lists and anxiety were simply gone. As if a movie montage, I saw every stressful situation in my life pop up in scenes all around me, one after another, from left to right.

And with each image, I heard the same message.

"You don't have to worry about people liking you so much. You don't have to worry about people liking you so much."

Over and over I heard this, and over and over I was discovering the root of my stress. I was worried about disappointing people, about losing their respect, worried about what they thought of me.

In that moment, I realized that I was often afraid to speak up for fear of not being liked. The scenes in the movie montage continued to bounce around my head. In one situation, I was embarrassed and ashamed, worried if someone would continue to respect me. In another situation, I was afraid to step forth and be bold with my opinions because I was afraid people wouldn't like me even if I were vocal. Do you see how many times I used the word "I" in those instances? Was I even looking at the power of the Lord at all in those situations?

This was a revelation. The pictures, the words and message were all so clear and so specific I knew this came from somewhere beyond my mind. After all, I've lived in my own mind for all these years and never had that clarity or perspective. Something new had entered the equation.

Do better. Improve. Rise up. Be the best. The list of personal faults that I needed to fix had dogged me for years. I was never good enough.

I thought this was normal, perhaps even a good thing. This is America after all. That day at the prayer center, I was hearing something else. *You are good enough. You are loved. You don't have to worry about screwing up. You are doing a good job and I will protect you.* A faint whisper. I was always so busy listening to another voice I had never heard the whisper.

I never knew I could hear from God. I wonder if all these years God was waiting for me to stop talking and to start listening.

I visited the prayer center every week for a month, asking question after question and receiving revelatory insight into the power of prayer and the words of the Bible over our thought lives. In those visits, the Bible sprang to life. It dawned on me that in all those years of suffering, I had been in the midst of a spiritual battle. My thought life was a war zone. Except I hadn't been fighting back. I suddenly understood the significance of the armor of God. 2 Corinthians 10:3-5, Ephesians 6:10-18.

I realized that I had allowed a spirit of fear, which the Bible tells us is not from God, to torment me for years. That spirit of fear planted thoughts and altered my perception of the world around me for so long that my mind started to believe I had reason to fear everything, all the time. A spirit of death, anger, perfectionism, pride, anxiety, depression, hopelessness, guilt and shame and even a Pharisaical spirit had been constant companions. I was complicit in believing the lies and permitting the thoughts to run rampant. And all those encounters with suicidal people? That was a spirit of suicide tormenting me. My mind resisted the temptation to think suicidal thoughts, yet the tormenting spirit caused fear and discouragement through those bizarre encounters I knew were more than a coincidence.

I learned we as believers have power in the name of Jesus Christ over these tormenting spirits. We hear in songs all the time that there is power in the name of Jesus, but it seems we never learn how to use it in a practical way. As believers we have the power of Jesus Christ living in us, and like the words spoken "in the beginning", our words, too, have power. "Fear, I command you to leave me in the name of Jesus Christ. You shall not return. Shame, you must leave me too.

Lord, fill me where I'm empty! Give me the mind of Christ" Mark 16:17-20, Philippians 2:9-11, 1 Corinthians 2:6-16. *Speak it out*!

The Bible says, "The name of the Lord is a fortified tower. The righteous run to it and are safe." Proverbs 18:10. Take this literally in those moments you are afraid or need extra comfort. Speak His name in your house, your car, even in a whisper at the mall or a restaurant or the gas station. Everywhere we go, we are safe in the power of His name.

I think back to the prayer in January of 2013, moving from the gray recliner to my knees on our cream-colored rug. That day, I didn't even have faith I could be healed from a hurting heart. I confessed the sin of unbelief, and asked the Lord to give me faith. And from that date onward, I see forward movement. Radical, life-altering movement, not necessarily on a schedule or with any predictability, but movement nonetheless. Real change. I'm inclined to think that in those years that I prayed without believing I could be healed, the Lord delighted even in the seeking. I think He was waiting for the right moment when He might nudge me closer to the place of whole-hearted devotion and belief.

We serve a generous God, one who is willing to overlook all sorts of errors when a person's heart inclines toward him. We serve a God who is waiting by our side for us to acknowledge Him in His incredible kindness and patience.

The Swing Set

All I wanted was for the pain to go away. I knew that was why I fell to my knees that day on the cream-colored rug. I had no illusions that life would be grand or exciting. That was no longer possible. And yet over the years after Rob died, an image persisted in my mind. It was an image of me as a little girl on the painted green swing set near our grove of trees on our farm in northwest Iowa.

On that swing set, I leaned back with my long, dark hair trailing like feathers and sweeping the gravel beneath me. I stared up at the trees and the clouds and felt a stirring in my soul. It was a promise of goodness. The unerring belief that God literally loved the whole world, from the trees above to the oldest person living on the farthest side of the world. I imagined busy people walking across a busy street in a busy city I'd never seen before. They were all in a hurry in a city so big it had traffic lights and lighted signs telling people when they could and could not cross. From my seat on the swing, I knew that God loved those people and that He wanted them to know it, too.

That was the best memory of my childhood. The warm sun, the breeze drawing its fingers through the tree leaves, and the glowing promise that there was good in store for everyone in the world.

When did I lose all that?

We took the kids to the park in Pennsylvania one summer evening, and I leaned back in the swing with eyes closed and my hair sweeping like a trail of feathers. I felt empty inside.

I thought back to those years of my youth and wept with regret that I had not realized then that those were good times. Mostly Rob and I wanted to be older or smarter or wiser, when all the while we were in the midst of glory and grace.

What was it about those days?

Our swing set, the one painted green, was destroyed along with our old farmhouse when the farmstead was gutted and burned to make room to grow more crops.

Was it really the swing set I was missing?

As a child, I was full of hope and trust. I believed. I believed God was with me as I sat on the swing set and I believed that at very same moment He was with those busy people walking the busy streets of the busy city on the farthest side of the world. I believed He was not only present and good, but He was also powerful. Powerful enough to transform the lives of all these people whom He loved.

The Bible tells us we are to have faith like a child. It tells us that Jesus had to command his contemporaries to let the children come to Him. We are told to become like children, and yet it seems ingrained in us that children are not prepared to experience God. We assume that as children we were naïve and unlearned, when the opposite is true. As children, we knew God as well as anybody.

The day of my first visit to the prayer center one of the women shared how she pictured me joyful and free on a swing with my hair trailing in the breeze. I was slow to catch on to the significance.

A few weeks later, I visited another prayer center in town where I prayed with a woman as another sat silently beside us doodling with a pencil on a yellow pad of paper. When we had finished, the other woman motioned for me to see her drawing.

My heart caught in my throat. In the margin at the top of the pad was a picture of a swing set, sunshine and cotton ball clouds. "What God says to you!" was written below. The drawing, without a doubt, was inspired by God speaking to this woman through the Holy Spirit. There is no other way to explain it. I had just met the two women and never mentioned a swing set.

With tears streaming down my face, I told the women of my search for the swing set and the peace and depth of emotion wrapped up in a childhood memory. "That's where the Lord met with you when you were a little girl," one of the women told me.

Everything shifted when she said this. It wasn't the swing set I was seeking all those years. No, I was seeking the peace and joy that I had as a little girl on that swing set. The peace and joy was a hand-in-glove companion to the God-is-powerful faith of my youth, and I realized when I lost the one I had lost the other.

In that moment, I knew beyond a shadow of a doubt the thoughts I had on the swing set were God-breathed truth: *He can* transform lives. He transformed mine. And when I saw the drawing of the swing set, He reminded me that He can transform the lives of *anyone* who comes to Him, no matter where or who they may be.

Instead of pursuing swing sets, now I pursue Him. When I still my spirit and think of Him with thankfulness, hopefulness and praise, the peace and joy bursts forth within me once again. I don't need the painted green swing set to experience His presence, because He is all around me, everywhere I go. He reminds me of this in the moment pieces of cotton seeds float in the sunlight streaming through the trees and time stands still for a few seconds, or when a high school choir sings "This Is My Father's World" at graduation. The song stirs something deep in my spirit.

"In the rustling grass, I hear him pass. He speaks to me everywhere." Indeed. Indeed He does.

~ ~ ~

I spoke earlier of desire. What did I want out of life? I can't help but think of those days on the swing set, hair streaming behind me, seeing the image of the busy people in the busy world burdened by cares. I desire to tell them it's all going to be okay. You don't have to worry. You don't have to fear. Our heavenly Father is closer than you think. He sees you. He knows you. And He wants good things for you.

As a child, I didn't have words or stories to prove it. I was just a little girl with a bursting heart.

All these years later, after chasing the wrong things and finding them empty and after seeing the darkness and fears many others face, I know with conviction we are in need. We are all in need.

While I may not know you or your circumstances, I can tell you after losing a brother, after feeling as if I lost my relationship with my parents, after working so hard with so little help for so long, after achieving everything and gaining nothing, and after trying to break free on my own and failing, I can still say that God is good. He loves you. And He is so near, waiting to reveal himself, if only you will seek Him with persistence and confidence believing He will be found.

The Gifts He Left Behind

My senior year of high school, Rob asked me to meet him at a varsity college basketball game in a nearby town. Rob wanted me to meet his new "friend." She was, he said, "a diamond in the rough."

She didn't look rough as we stood together on the basketball court, the crowd streaming out around us after the game. In fact, she looked like she might be his girlfriend. She was a beautiful, quiet-spirited farm girl whom Rob met a few weeks after she started college.

In November of 1999, an airline offered a killer deal on a three-day stay in Bangkok, Thailand, where a family friend worked for a software company. My parents along with Rob and I and our significant others traveled the twenty-plus hours to Thailand where we harvested rice, watched a kickboxing match, played with orphan children in a nearby village and rode elephants.

It was in Thailand that Rob bought the fake Polo Ralph Lauren belt he would one day wear in his casket. And it was in Thailand Rob gave his then-girlfriend the nickname "Cooner," a play on the Thai word for friend.

Rob and Cooner were married in June of 2001. Rob was late for wedding photos because he was shooting hoops that morning with friends. Cooner was unflustered by his late arrival. She understood and loved Rob just as he was.

It was she who called my mom the morning of July 17, 2005, through panic and tears telling her to come over, that Rob had hurt himself. She was the one who found him.

A few years after their wedding, Rob and I stood together in the lobby of Minerva's Restaurant in downtown Sioux Falls, along with Cooner, my parents, my husband, and my in-laws. We stood along a wall with a fish tank, watching goldfish swimming, when Rob leaned over and whispered to me, "Cooner's pregnant....but you can't tell anyone yet." Oh Rob, life was never dull with you around.

Rob and Cooner's son was born in June of 2004.

In high school, Rob was close friends with two brothers, one a year older and the other a year younger than him. The two brothers were Rob's basketball teammates. They were like family to Rob and me. After high school basketball games, Rob and I visited their grandparents' house for homemade ice cream, that sort of thing.

After Rob died, the older brother felt a strong commitment to helping raise Rob's son. He loved him because he was Rob's. The older brother started spending more and more time with Rob's son and also with Cooner in the years after Rob's death.

The older brother and Cooner were married on August 2007, in a destination wedding in Myrtle Beach, South Carolina. A baby girl followed a few years later, and a set of twins are now on the way. We love them and claim them as family, as if we were all of one blood. We are tied together by more than tragedy and by more than the memory of the person who first brought us together all those years ago. I am tied to them because through the midst of a great tragedy, I saw their true substance, and I saw that it is good. It is very good. They exemplify patience, grace and mercy. They bear witness to the power of Christ to carry believers through tragedy and to keep us free of bitterness and resentment.

We see them at holidays, or when we go for dinner together or when we watch Rob's son play basketball, just like Rob. He played at the fourth grade level when only in second grade. Rob would be so proud of him.

He Will Die. Share His Story.

My mom is the youngest of thirteen children. Her father died when she was not yet a year old. She and her siblings managed the family farm to survive. Money was not plentiful.

In the summer of 1972, my mom heard about a gathering for young people in Dallas, Texas. This gathering, Explo '72, featured speaker Billy Graham. Nearly one hundred thousand youth from all across the nation were drawn to Dallas to attend. This event is considered the most visible moment of the 1970's Jesus Movement.

A group from northwest Iowa organized a bus trip to Dallas for Explo '72. My mom heard about the bus trip and event on a local radio station. Something internal propelled her to join them. "I am supposed to go," she thought. A boldness overtook my mom and she made the phone call to reserve a spot on the bus for herself and her sister.

She said something inside her told her that she didn't need to worry about the cost. She knew the Lord would provide the funds she needed. To pay their way, she and her sister "picked rock" in a neighbor's field in scorching heat, working until the evening before the bus departed. The trip to Explo '72 was the first and only time my mother traveled any distance from home.

I heard this story for the first time a few weeks ago. We were talking with a man who is helping organize a revival event on the National Mall in July of 2016. He said the event was going to be "like Explo '72." "Oh yeah," my mom said. "I remember Explo. I was there." I do not exaggerate when I tell you I almost fell over in surprise. As soon as we were out of earshot, I asked her how in the world she ended up on a bus trip to Dallas for what some consider to be a sort of Christian Woodstock. After all, she was a shy Iowa farm girl who didn't have much money.

"It was like there was something inside me drawing me to go," she said.

For many reasons her story struck me, perhaps most significantly because it shows that even in her teenage years my mom was hearing the Lord speak to her.

~ ~ ~

Three years before Rob died, my mom stood in the kitchen of our home in northwest Iowa, praying for someone whom she knew was suffering from suicidal thoughts. As she prayed, a singular thought flashed through her mind. "It won't be [that person]. Rob is the one who's going to take his life." The message was so clear and direct that my mom fell forward onto the kitchen counter in disbelief.

What she heard next is what made this book possible at all. It is the reason my otherwise private family is okay with me sharing all of this. She next heard, "Someday I want you to talk about it to help others."

She never told our family she had heard this.

A year-and-a-half ago, I told my mom I desired to write a book that included Rob's story, but before I started I wanted to make sure our family was okay with it. She said yes, and shared what she had held inside all those years.

In that phone call I began to understand my mother's stoic strength following my brother's death. It is a stoicism that at times angered and confused me in the years after Rob died.

In the three years between the day my mom heard the Lord speak to her in the kitchen and the day Rob took his life, my mom wrestled with what she heard. She interceded in prayer and she took every step she thought might prevent Rob's death. And yet.

And yet he died.

My mom shared how she lived with the burden of this information for all those years until Rob's death. At times she wondered if she had misheard; Rob's spirit would lift and then crash, lift and crash. Each time his spirit lifted, hope stirred in my mom's heart that perhaps Rob would not take his life.

But as the years progressed, my mom could tell Rob's spirit was slipping away. She could tell we were losing him. Darkness was strengthening its foothold. On her days off work she sometimes spent all day praying for Rob. She stayed up into the night, asking the Lord to have mercy and save Rob from the darkness that was swallowing him. Mom shared how a few months before Rob died, she felt her spirit surrender, and the darkness was lifted from her. She knew. She knew Rob was not doing well, and, in fact, that he was going downhill. In spite of this, she felt peace. She shared how she grieved all those years before Rob's death.

On the morning of July 17, 2005, the day Rob died, my mom was at peace knowing the Lord was in control. He was not asleep at the wheel.

The Winning Ticket

Three days ago, for the second time in my life, I played the lottery. The Powerball® jackpot is at a record high. I'm usually oblivious to anything lottery-related, but every time I saw a headline about the Powerball, it grabbed my attention. My eyes were drawn to the headlines time and time again in a noticeable way.

"Lord," I asked, "please show me why these articles are drawing my attention." As soon as I prayed this prayer, a singular thought came to mind: Buy a ticket.

I grew up in a home where gambling, dancing and drinking were taboo. "Lord, this doesn't sound like the God of my church, and yet it does sound like the God of the Bible who told Haggai to marry an adulterous woman. I can't predict how you're going to work, other than to know that your ways are unusual. Please show me if this is you." I decided to draw lots, a Bible-based practice of committing a seemingly random drawing of "yes/no" to God to discern His will.

I wrote the words "yes" and "no" on two small pieces of paper as I sat in my car waiting to pick up my daughter from school. I shook the two pieces of paper in my cupped hands. I drew a "yes."

So I bought a ticket. As I waited in line, I saw the man in front of me, too, was buying a ticket. He looked destitute. He was rail-thin, his shoulder blades protruding from his shabby, soiled work coat. As he turned from the counter to walk out the door, his head was held low as if he felt invisible and was trying to make himself so. I felt there was pain inside him. And yet I perceived that this man in many ways was rich, for he still believed in miracles. For him, I could see that a miracle was all he had to hope for.

After I bought the ticket, I felt a wave of excitement. For so long, perhaps my entire life, I've felt a deep sense of anticipation; a belief that like the man buying the lottery ticket, I too will see a big-deal miracle in my lifetime. "This might be the miracle," I thought.

The winning numbers were announced last night. I did not win.

I felt at peace, and yet my heart was broken. "Lord," I said through tears, "what are you trying to tell me through this?" I said many more things from a place of deep pain and disappointment, reflecting on all these years of my life where I've hoped and waited to no avail. "Will I ever see miracles as in times of old?"

As I prayed, it occurred to me that perhaps I'm not alone. It occurred to me all creation groans alongside me with the desire to see evidence of God's goodness when all around seems not.

As I prayed, I thought, too of a conversation I overheard recently about the doctrine of "election," an ongoing discussion in the church of how God chooses who is saved and who is not saved. I thought about the man standing in line buying the lottery ticket, and I wondered what he would have thought if he could hear Christians talk about this. Would he have felt loved? Would he have felt invited? Do we as the church believe that a man like him, destitute and desperate, is a person of the sort who is invited to enter the kingdom of God? Of course we would say yes, but do we really believe it?

As I prayed and as I thought of the lottery, the doctrine of election, hope, dejection, anticipation and discouragement, I saw the image of Jesus handing out lottery tickets. I saw Him standing on a street corner in a city handing them out to every single person who passed by. I saw Him wading waist-deep through vast swaths of wheat fields to hand a ticket to a lone farmer standing by a tractor in the middle of nowhere. I saw Him in slums on the far sides of the world handing tickets to shoeless, shirtless children who gathered around Him in hungering excitement. I saw Him in London in Parliament handing tickets to men and women in bespoke suits. He was handing tickets to every single person in the world.

Every ticket was a winning ticket. They were all winners.

All the person had to do was call the number on the back to claim the jackpot. Simple.

Yet I saw some take the ticket and cast it aside as if it were a scrap of junk mail. I saw some take the ticket and pause, considering whether to call, then waving off the phone call until later. I saw some looking at the number, picking up the phone, but calling someone else, a non-lottery official representing a false god, calling a different number and rejecting the opportunity to claim the prize through the phone number printed on the ticket. I saw some break down in tears, weeping at the thought that they might become rich, yet believing they were born to be poor; because of everything that had ever happened to them they believed they were not good enough to claim this prize.

Oh, my dear friend, I speak to you today. Claim your ticket. Call the number on the back. There is only one number, and its numbers on the dial pad spell "J-E-S-U-S." In His name, all things are possible. In His name, we claim riches.

~ ~ ~

The actual Powerball offers either a lifetime annuity or lump sum. Our winning tickets offer both the lifetime annuity and a lump sum.

The lifetime annuity varies for each person. Some are given greater material provision than others, which may cause disappointment, comparison and thoughts of unfairness that must be overcome in order to fully enjoy the annuity we each receive.

All of us receive equal, ample non-material provision. We have unlimited phone access to call the number on the back anytime and to talk as long as we want. We have no guarantees of how often the voice on the other end will speak, which can be maddening at times and that, too, must be overcome.

Yet the ticket provides ample written instruction and encouragement: God's Word, the Bible. This Word can be overwhelming and confusing at times, and yet I know from personal experience if you ask to understand the Word and ask Him to speak to you through His Word, He will do it.

The lump sum is the same for all of us. The lump sum is unlimited supply of everything we've ever longed for, and it is awarded when we pass on from this world. The lump sum is residence in our heavenly home.

Powerball winnings are taxable. Ours are not. Do not permit shame, fear, doubt, greed, confusion, disappointment or any other temptation let you settle for less than the full amount of your prize. Refuse to let the enemy tax your winnings. Stand firm in Jesus' powerful name and pray like your joy depends on it, because it does.

~ ~ ~

Rob suffered much before he died. He was spiritually, mentally and physically oppressed. Perhaps the oppression started because he was so focused on the lump sum that he couldn't enjoy the lifetime annuity. I told you he was obsessed with heaven in an unhealthy way. Perhaps Rob's oppression was a torment permitted as in the book of Job. Or perhaps the Lord was setting the stage for a miracle in Rob's life, just as when the Lord put it in Pharaoh's heart to set out and chase the Israelites after they were set free, to set the stage for the parting of the Red Sea and the annihilation of Israel's tormenters. Exodus 14:8. Whatever the reason, Rob was tormented and it hurts to think of the pain he and so many like him have endured.

The Bible says that the world will reach a point where wrong is glorified as right, and I see this lately in the context of suicide. Isaiah 5:20, 2 Timothy 3. People claim suicide is heroic or valiant or what have you. The Bible tells me Rob's final act was wrong. Suicide is a sin. I told you that after Satan entered Judas and he betrayed Jesus, Judas' next act was to take his life. Do not be deceived by thoughts of suicide. Know the source of the thoughts.

The Bible upholds life. It says "Do you not know that your bodies are temples of the Holy Spirit, who is in you, whom you have received from God? You are not your own; you were bought at a price. Therefore honor God with your bodies." 1 Corinthians 6:19-20. And Jeremiah 1:5 tells us, "Before I formed you in the womb I knew you, before you were born I set you apart." And if you need more proof we are loved and our lives are precious, Psalm 139:13 says, " For you created my inmost being; you knit me together in my mother's womb." Let us never forget that our life is a gift no matter how bleak it seems at the moment. If you can't see the value of your existence, ask God to show you. He will tell you if you are willing to listen.

Suicide is a sin that causes tremendous pain and fallout for those left behind. It is wrong in every way even though its temptation may sound right to those who are hurting. Even so, it is a sin that is forgiven.

The Bible tells us the requirements for salvation. "If you declare with your mouth, 'Jesus is Lord,' and believe in your heart that God raised him from the dead, you will be saved." Romans 10:9.

Belief in Jesus is an absolute requirement for salvation. Jesus' name is the number on the back of that ticket and that number is the one and only number that works. Some will think it is arrogant of me to say there is only one number to call. I am sorry to offend, but I must speak truth or my insides will curdle. The Bible says, "Whoever believes in the Son has eternal life, but whoever rejects the Son will not see life, for God's wrath remains on them." John 3:36. We are told to look for practical evidence of this belief. "This is to my Father's glory, that you bear much fruit, showing yourselves to be my disciples." John 15:8.

You may wonder why I include the story of the Powerball ticket. It is this: I want for you to meet Rob and I want to meet you, too. You see, Rob is in heaven. Rob declared Jesus as his Lord and Savior during his lifetime. He expressed his belief that God raised Jesus from the dead. And his life bore much fruit, from his influence on me to the woman who met him once for fifteen minutes and on whom he made an unforgettable impression. Because of this, I believe Rob has an eternal home in heaven. We look forward to seeing him again, and hope you will be there with us to meet him.

~ ~ ~

Like Rob, I lost my way for awhile, too. I see that now. My grief and pride in self had become an idol, standing between me and my Lord. I was too proud to call the number and to claim the lifetime annuity, to claim the healing that the Lord wanted for me. But the idols of grief and pride were obliterated when I confessed my sin and repented that day on the plush cream rug on my living room floor and healing came forth.

John the Baptist, preparing the way for Jesus, said, "Repent, for the Kingdom of Heaven has come near." Matthew 3:2. I used to read this verse and feel scared, like I was in trouble and there was nothing I could do about it because I continually failed in my attempts to be a perfect person. But that's not the truth.

We don't use the word "repent" that often in everyday language. It's simple really. Repent simply means "to change one's mind."

Acts 3:19 tells us repentance is a good thing: "Repent, then, and turn to God, so that your sins may be wiped out, *that times of refreshing may come from the Lord.*"

I changed my mind that day on the plush cream rug. I was incorrect in believing God could not heal me and in believing His plan was not good. In that moment on the rug I changed my mind, choosing to believe that He was powerful enough to heal me and that His plan was good even though all around me appeared hopeless. As the Bible promised, refreshment indeed followed. God always keeps His promises.

~ ~ ~

Claim the lifetime annuity every single day. Every single day we call that phone number and we repent, every single day, asking the Lord to reveal anything standing between Him and us. And in those areas where we continually relapse into old thoughts and behaviors, we tell Him we want to think rightly and act rightly, but can't do it on our own. "Lord, I need your help. Without you I am powerless to change."

In confessing our weakness and our need to Him every day, we make more and more room for the Lord to dwell in us through the Holy Spirit.

And we forgive every single day. Unforgiveness is the static on the phone line between us and God. Or for the cell phone generation, unforgiveness causes limited reception. We hear Him clearly and we make room for the fullness of God's love in us when we forgive.

Forgiveness. I haven't told you about forgiveness. I struggle to share it because it was so painful.

The day I prayed with the two women and one drew a picture of the swing set, we invested a chunk of time praying forgiveness over various people in my life. I started by asking the Lord to show me anyone I needed to forgive. I told the woman every person who came to my mind. The list was long. Finally I said I was finished. No one else came to mind. The woman praying with me said, "There are two people you haven't mentioned."

I couldn't figure out who that might be.

"Your brother and yourself," she said.

I thought I had forgiven Rob, but knew this was not true because my insides heaved when she suggested I forgive him. How could I forgive Rob? He didn't say good-bye to me in his suicide note. He never said good-bye. He killed himself when he was only twenty-seven. We were supposed to grow old alongside one another. He was supposed to join me at my kids' graduations, their weddings. He broke this unspoken promise to me. It took everything inside me to forgive him. When I said the words, "Lord, I forgive my brother Rob," I tasted the salt of the tears in my mouth. I felt shaken, yet my spirit knew something had changed for the better.

Next, I forgave myself. This was just as difficult. In my mind I did not deserve forgiveness. In my mind, I was a failure in every way. I did not live up to my own expectations. I was weak. I could not make it through the pain on my own. Even though I didn't feel I deserved forgiveness, I made my mouth speak the words. "I forgive myself, and I ask you, Lord, to bless me." Again, I felt shaken, yet my spirit knew something had changed for the better.

It occurred to me sometime later that forgiveness is really a matter of, "Who is God in our lives?" When I asked God for His forgiveness so many months before, repenting of my unbelief and pride on the plush cream rug, He washed me clean of my sins. He remembered them no more. Yet I would not forgive myself. I was saying, in effect, even if He has forgiven me, I choose to hold myself hostage for my past.

Please, don't make the same mistake I did. Do not hold yourself in bondage for sins that are no longer there. "It is for freedom that Christ has set us free. Stand firm, then, and do not let yourselves be burdened again by a yoke of slavery." Galatians 5:1. If He has forgiven us, then we are free.

~ ~ ~

Forgiveness, confession and repentance. Write these words down. Commit to making them a daily practice. And when you have done so, "May God himself, the God of peace, sanctify you through and through. May your whole spirit, soul and body be kept blameless at the coming of our Lord Jesus Christ. The one who calls you is faithful and he will do it." 1 Thessalonians 5:23-24.

He will do it.

~ ~ ~

The lifetime annuity doesn't always look that appealing. The voice on the other end of the line may call us to step out in faith in ways that don't make sense in our limited understanding.

For example, we may buy a lottery ticket on faith and end up without even a single number that matches. In doing the things that seem foolish, stand on the belief that obedience is a fragrant offering to God. As a friend in the Lord reminds me again and again, to obey is better than to sacrifice. 1 Samuel 15:22.

We must stand on belief that everything we are called to do bears fruit when we step out in obedience, because our understanding is limited. "For the foolishness of God is wiser than human wisdom, and the weakness of God is stronger than human strength....But God chose the foolish things of the world to shame the wise; God chose the weak things of the world to shame the strong." 1 Corinthians 1:25-27.

~ ~ ~

When you claim that winning ticket, be prepared for challenges. Before Jesus ascended to heaven, He said "Peace I leave with you; my peace I give to you." John 14:27. But He also said, "I did not come to bring peace, but a sword." Matthew 10:34. Not a literal sword, for He rebuked Peter when Peter took up a sword in His defense at the Garden of Gethsemane. Matthew 26:52. The sword is one of division, separating us from everything we once clung to as security; careers, financial stability, reputation, even our loved ones.

I keep quoting scripture. I can't help it. Truth is truth. "Most certainly I tell you, unless a grain of wheat falls into the earth and dies, it remains by itself alone. But if it dies, it bears much fruit. He who loves his life will lose it. He who hates his life in this world will keep it to eternal life." John 12:24-25. Jesus also tells us "whoever loses his life for my sake will find it." Matthew 10:39.

I was called to relinquish my career and in turn my misplaced identity, to relinquish anger at my father, and even to relinquish grief over Rob's death. The process can feel unsettling. Rob might have called it discombobulating. I gave up every perceived right to control my life. It was in the giving up that I received. In dying to myself I learned to live.

~ ~ ~

For so long, I regretted my fight with Rob the evening before he died. "If only!" I thought time and time again. There came a time when I knew I had to let go of regret. I prayed and asked the Lord to settle the matter for me once and for all. As I prayed, it occurred to me God was in control of Rob's life and the timing of his death. Even though I spoke angrily to Rob the night before he died, the Lord was the one in charge and not me. I did not need to carry responsibility for the fight that evening. I was forgiven for treating Rob harshly.

Another thought sprung up: Oh, if only I had walked closer to the Lord during that time. If only I had set my mind to gain understanding and had humbled myself before the Lord so that I might have seen breakthrough in Rob's life. I know it would have happened. Yet I did not walk rightly with God at that time and so I knew I had to ask for, and claim, God's forgiveness for this sin.

I believe Rob could have been healed. It would have been no big deal for the Lord to heal Rob. I see that now.

So why did God not reveal the fullness of Himself to my family before Rob died? Why did we not know then what we know now about spiritual oppression and the power of the Holy Spirit to purify our minds of those thoughts? The Lord could have shown our family before, but He didn't. I don't know why, and it's taken me years to be okay with this. Some days His timing confuses me. Some days His timing frustrates me. Many days I feel like a bridled horse chomping at the bit to run on ahead of God, yet I know without that bridle I run the wrong direction every single time. Every day I must stand on the belief His timing is best.

Yes, in His time He is the one who softens hearts and convicts of sin. Yes, in His time He is the one who reveals the mysteries in His Word.

Yet we are part and parcel of God's timing and movement. Daniel the prophet from the Bible, fasted and received a powerful vision sent by a messenger who was released from the heavens to visit him. The messenger said, "Since the first day that you *set your mind* to gain understanding and to humble yourself before your God, your words were heard, and I have come in response to them." Daniel 10:12.

Before Rob died, I spoke out that I was a follower of Christ, yet I had not set my mind to it. And because I had not set my mind to it, I suffered greatly. Oh the peace I missed out on! Please, don't be like me. Don't be a follower in word only. Set your mind to gaining understanding and to humbling yourself before God. He will show up just like He did for Daniel. In fact, for those of you who now resolve to set your mind on Him, He's already on His way.

~ ~ ~

As a little girl, I had a favorite Bible verse. In it, the Lord said to His people as they prepared to enter the Promised Land, "Have I not commanded you? Be strong and courageous. Do not be afraid; do not be discouraged, for the Lord your God will be with you wherever you go." Joshua 1:9.

As a little girl, I saw this verse as a warm and cuddly blanket of encouragement. Like God was saying, "Please, try it this way."

I read this verse so many years later, and I see it in a new way. This verse is more than a suggestion. It is more than an encouragement. It is a command. He commands it because He loves us and wants the best for us.

We need boundaries. We need a healthy respect of the Lord's commands because without it we are about as safe a piece of paper blowing about in a billowing furnace, at any time about to be consumed by the raging fire of our culture and our weak flesh. His commands are to keep us safe from the wiles of the enemy. I see that now because I was almost burned alive.

God knows our fears just like He knew the fears of Joshua and His people. When Joshua spied out the land, he reported back to the Israelites that the land was incredible. It flowed with milk and honey. But giants stood in the way. If the people focused on the giants, they would succumb to fear and discouragement, and would miss out on the best in store for them.

Before they crossed over the Jordan, at least five times the Lord commanded Joshua and his troops to be strong and courageous, not to fear or to grow discouraged, "for the Lord your God will be with you wherever you go."

This promise was fulfilled, like every single promise and prophecy in the Bible, for after they crossed the Jordan River into the Promised Land, the Lord personally revealed Himself to Joshua. Joshua 5:14-15.

Like Joshua and the Israelites, the lifetime annuity guarantees us our own Promised Land: the fruit of the Spirit. The fruit of the Spirit is love, joy, peace, patience, kindness, goodness, faithfulness, gentleness and self-control. Galatians 5:22-23.

The giants in our way are fear, doubt, hopelessness and all the other forms of darkness that manifest in our world today.

Only light repels darkness, and Jesus is the way, the truth, and the light. John 14:6. *Call on His name.* Speak it out whenever and wherever you are to remind yourself He is here. Don't focus on the darkness swirling around you. Focus on the power of the light.

~ ~ ~

I know now that the promise of the Lord's presence remains true today, for all who believe. The swing set proved it to me. The Lord was with me on the swing set in the days of my youth. And He showed me in the drawing of the swing set that He is still with me so many years later. He was always with me and He always will be.

~ ~ ~

Our family's favorite television show was Columbo, starring Peter Falk as a bumbling yet brilliant detective. Lieutenant Columbo was famous for popping his head back in the door one last time, to the point of annoyance, to ask one last question. "Just one more thing," he always said.

I have just one more thing to share.

The Lord prompts me almost every day to read Jeremiah 10:23-24. In this verse the prophet Jeremiah says, "I know, O Lord, that a man's life is not his own; it is not for man to direct his steps. Correct me, Lord, but only with justice—not in your anger, lest you reduce me to nothing." This is one of the most powerful passages in the Bible. It is the story of my life in two sentences. It is the story of all our lives.

Jesus once healed a group of ten lepers of their physical ailment. Only one of the ten lepers returned to thank Him. The Bible says that the man who returned in thankfulness was the only one of the ten who was "made well," meaning he received a spiritual blessing, a fullness of life, in addition to the physical healing. Luke 17:11-19.

It would be nice to receive a spiritual blessing. An even stronger impetus for giving thanks, though, is that through all the pain and loneliness, Jesus was always there for me. He corrected me with justice, not in anger. He is my friend. I love Him.

The Catalyst, Revisited

I told you way back at the beginning of this book I asked to see God at work in my life. He honored my request. The stories in this book testify to it.

I told you way back at the beginning of this book that I might not have survived what was to follow if God had not opened my eyes.

You see, what followed was so much more than what I've shared thus far. There was more. A few months after verbalizing the desire to see God at work in my life, my entire life was catalyzed into tumult and uncertainty.

My husband unknowingly contracted the mono virus and started showing symptoms the day of our wedding. I spent our honeymoon wandering around alone in Breckenridge, Colorado, while he slept all day in our hotel room. I wasn't even old enough to drive the rental car.

A few weeks after recovering from mono, he suffered an appendix attack and underwent an emergency appendectomy. It occurred during a two-week span in which our medical insurance had lapsed. We only later discovered we qualified for gap insurance coverage.

A few months after this, at the age of 21, I discovered we were pregnant with our first child. I sat for the LSAT not more than a week or two after learning I was pregnant, fighting waves of nausea and panic, fearful of whether it would work to have a baby in law school at what should have been the most joyous of times.

My husband and I have been married for over fifteen years, and we can tell you story after story of the mountains we've climbed together.

This is the tip of the iceberg. From the day I spoke out those words, the change was fast, furious and unrelenting. Fifteen years of climbing mountains. When we ask God for revelation, we are tested. We go through the fire.

People have all sorts of notions about what God does and does not do. Is He good because He doesn't want bad things to happen to us and the bad things only happen because God is involved from a distance? Is He not good because bad things do happen?

I say to you this: I would not trade one test or one trial, because when we suffer we share in the sufferings of Christ. 2 Corinthians 1:5. Without suffering, how hard it is to have desperate need of Him. Without coming to the edge of ourselves, we believe we are limitless.

I have suffered, yet I still believe God is good. I only know He is good because He opened my eyes to His work in my life and in the world around me.

~ ~ ~

But he said to me, "My grace is sufficient for you, my power is made perfect in weakness." Therefore I will boast all the more gladly about my weaknesses, so that Christ's power may rest on me. That is why, for Christ's sake, I delight in weaknesses, in insults, in hardships, in persecutions, in difficulties. For when I am weak, then I am strong. ~ 2 Corinthians 12:9-10.

Now It Springs Up

Two friends recently shared that when they prayed for me they heard the word "peace." My heart perked up in expectation, and I told each of them how a few days earlier I had purchased a throw pillow at Target® with the word *"peace"* written on it in burnished copper paillettes. As I put it in the cart, I asked the Lord to pour out His peace over my family .

Yes, I believe my family is entering a season of peace.

I think of the days of my youth, hair trailing in the breeze as I leaned back in the swing. Oh, how I remember that season of my life when all around me was peaceful. Oh, how I remember the firm conviction deep inside me that all things would end well because God is good.

As my story winds to an end, I wonder if the season of peace has already come. Reflecting on the words I spoke at the tender age of 19, talking that afternoon with my then-fiancé and now-husband, I know that God heard me that day. He has shown me so much of who He is, and the more I see of Him I can't help but feel at peace. How could I not? I know that I am heard, understood and cared for by someone exceedingly powerful and good.

Yes, we have faced trials of many kinds, but I believe what is in store for my family is extraordinarily good. It is a new thing.

Twenty-nine words have kept me afloat these last few years: "See, I am doing a new thing! Now it springs up; do you not perceive it? I am making a way in the wilderness and streams in the wasteland." Isaiah 43:19.

No matter our past or present circumstances, let us never forget that God does new things. Surprises pop up out of nowhere. Relief comes when we least expect it from a source we never imagined. If you haven't seen good from your trials yet, take heart. He is doing a new thing in you and for you, and He will reveal it to you if you ask Him.

~ ~ ~

I remain confident of this: I will see the goodness of the Lord in the land of the living. Wait for the Lord; be strong and take heart and wait for the Lord.
~ Psalm 27:13-14.

Epilogue

Rob
October 21, 1977 - July 17, 2005

In the summertime, before our daily nap, Grandma Leta read Rob and me a story. One afternoon, we sat enraptured at her feet as she read "Hot as Summer, Cold as Winter," the story of a listless king who challenges his staff and subjects to present him a dessert as hot as summer and as cold as winter. To the delight of the king and the chagrin of the king's chefs, a young boy wins the challenge with a hot fudge sundae.

In high school, Rob and I drove through the McDonald's drive-thru when one was near, ordering a hot fudge sundae with nuts. Rob finished it off by tilting the plastic cup back, slurping the remainder and licking out the hot fudge with a sweep of his tongue around the rim.

Cooner, Rob's widow, says Rob always begged her to ride bike with him to Dairy Queen. She protested every time, yet Rob always prevailed some way, somehow. Inevitably she found herself on a bike halfway to Dairy Queen.

This summer and fall were marked by an unusually frequent number of visits to Dairy Queen, oftentimes five visits per week, sometimes even two visits in one day. I went through the drive-thru today, in fact.

My husband (Dirksen, as Rob called him and who appeared kind the moment I first saw him), orders a Peanut Buster Parfait. After eating half, he would always offer me the remainder, claiming to be full. It finally occurred to me this summer, after fifteen years of marriage, that he can handily down the whole thing by himself. He's only offering me half to be kind. Sometimes first impressions are spot-on.

And so now I order my own cool treat. I discovered a few months ago that a small hot fudge sundae with peanuts is essentially a miniature Peanut Buster Parfait. I've made this my new dessert of choice.

Rachel, who chased after Rob with the big, red playground ball the night before he died, is now fourteen. She is the most adventurous of the bunch, regularly trying new Blizzard flavors, although a staid favorite is a brownie batter Blizzard with chocolate ice cream.

Kate, who shared with me her dream of Rob coming back, is almost ten. She orders two plain cheeseburgers.

And Brynn, who slept in the crib while I cried in my closet making the decision to leave the law firm, is four-and-a-half. She loves herself a cotton candy Blizzard. Those are now out of season and we are working hard to find her a new favorite.

On the best of summer evenings, you will find our family out for ice cream after one of my nephew's baseball games, along with my parents, Cooner and the older brother whom she married. On these evenings I know God is near. It is by His grace we have one another. And it is by His grace we will see our beloved Rob again someday.

~ ~ ~

--the people living in darkness
have seen a great light;
on those living in the land of the shadow of death
a light has dawned.

~As prophesied of Jesus and recounted in Matthew 4:16.

More about THE SWING SET

Visit **strongrightarm.com** for video interviews with me, my friends and family, and other information about *The Swing Set*.

Peace and Salvation

If you have questions about faith in Jesus Christ, here are a few resources:

The Billy Graham Evangelistic Association ("BGEA") shares direction and encouragement for your pursuit of the Way, the Truth, and the Life through Jesus Christ. Visit the BGEA website at **http://billygraham.org/grow-your-faith/** for more information.

The Christian Broadcasting network ("CBN"--Yes, that CBN), provides helpful information similar to BGEA, at **http://www.cbn.com/stepstopeace/**.

Personal Prayer

If you have a personal prayer request, please contact Direct Line Prayer Center, the prayer center mentioned in *The Swing Set*. It is a multi-denominational Christian prayer center staffed by volunteer prayer ministers. Who knows? I may even answer the line!

877. 717.8054 (national/toll free)

605.274.9274 (local)

For online information, visit **www.directlinesd.org**.

The Sioux Falls Healing Rooms in Sioux Falls, South Dakota, offers prayer similar to Direct Line Prayer Center.

www.siouxfallshealingrooms.com/

605.496.4795

Mental Health/Suicide Prevention Resources

In South Dakota

The Helpline Center operates the 24/7 suicide prevention and crisis line at 1.800.273.8255 (same as the national number).

You may also dial 211 in Sioux Falls or find information online at **helplinecenter.org**.

In the U.S.

National Suicide Prevention Lifeline - 1.800.273.8255 (A Nationwide 24/7 Suicide Prevention and Crisis Line)

For online information, visit **www.suicidepreventionlifeline.org** or **www.afsp.org**.

International

The International Association of Suicide Prevention has a list of international crisis center hotline numbers and chat services. Visit **www.iasp.info** for more information.

Please do your own research in addition to considering these resources. I cannot guarantee the accuracy or helpfulness of the phone numbers or website information as applied to your exact situation.